ST. NORBERT COLLEGE
309.1597 C76p
Conference on Social Development
Problems of freedom

D1624911

11 8

309.1597
C76p

WITHDRAWN

CONFERENCE ON SOCIAL DEVELOPMENT AND WELFARE IN
" VIETNAM

PROBLEMS
OF
FREEDOM

South Vietnam
Since Independence

Edited by Wesley R. Fishel

Introduction by Senator Mike Mansfield

The Contributors:
Joseph Buttinger
John C. Donnell
John T. Dorsey, Jr.
Wesley R. Fishel
William Henderson
John B. Hendry
Wolf Ladejinsky
Craig S. Litchenwalner, M.D.
Tran Ngoc Lien
Robert R. Nathan
Edgar N. Pike
Vu Van Thai

THE FREE PRESS OF GLENCOE, INC.
A Division of the Crowell-Collier Publishing Company, New York

BUREAU OF SOCIAL AND POLITICAL RESEARCH
Michigan State University, East Lansing

131784

309.1597
C76p

Copyright © 1961
By the Board of Trustees of Michigan State University
East Lansing, Michigan
Library of Congress
Catalog Card Number: 61-62517

25 June 62
McClurg
4.87
Carnegie

TABLE OF CONTENTS

Foreword   by Wesley R. Fishel   v

Introduction   by the Hon. Mike Mansfield, United States Senate   ix

Chapter 1   THE CONSEQUENCES OF PARTITION   1
                by Robert R. Nathan

Chapter 2   PROBLEMS OF DEMOCRATIC GROWTH
                    IN FREE VIETNAM   9
                by Wesley R. Fishel

Chapter 3   PERSONALISM IN VIETNAM   29
                by John C. Donnell

Chapter 4   VIETNAM'S CONCEPT OF DEVELOPMENT   69
                by Vu Van Thai

Chapter 5   PROBLEMS OF EDUCATION IN VIETNAM   75
                by Edgar N. Pike

Chapter 6   THE ETHNIC MINORITIES IN THE REPUBLIC
                    OF VIETNAM   99
                by Joseph Buttinger

Chapter 7   OPENING OF NEW LANDS AND VILLAGES:
                    THE REPUBLIC OF VIETNAM'S
                    LAND DEVELOPMENT PROGRAM   123
                by William Henderson

Chapter 8   STRESSES AND STRAINS IN A DEVELOPING
                    ADMINISTRATIVE SYSTEM   139
                by John T. Dorsey, Jr.

Chapter 9   AGRARIAN REFORM IN THE REPUBLIC
                    OF VIETNAM   153
                by Wolf I. Ladejinsky

Chapter 10   THE GROWTH OF AGRICULTURAL CREDIT AND
                    COOPERATIVES IN VIETNAM   177
                by Tran Ngoc Lien

Chapter 11   THE SOCIAL AND ECONOMIC CHARACTERISTICS
                    OF THE WORK FORCE IN SAIGON   191
                by James B. Hendry

Appendix I   TABULAR DATA ON THE CHARACTERISTICS
              OF THE WORK FORCE IN SAIGON   206
              by James B. Hendry

Appendix II   LIMITATIONS OF THE SURVEY OF THE
              CHARACTERISTICS OF THE WORK FORCE
              IN SAIGON   216
              by James B. Hendry

Appendix III HEALTH PROGRESS IN VIETNAM   219
              by Craig S. Lichtenwalner, M.D.

Index   —

LIST OF MAPS

American Assistance Since 1953 to June 1959
    Under Education Projects   79
Expansion and Improvement of Technical Vocational Education   86
Distribution of Ethnic Groups in Vietnam (Simplified)   98
Land Development (Rural Resettlement), June, 1959   131
Agrarian Reform Area Subject to Transfer, June, 1959   167
The National Agricultural Credit Office NACO, June, 1959   179
Agricultural Cooperatives, June, 1959   183
Improved Irrigation and Water Control, June, 1959   185
Improvement of Nursing and Allied Education, June, 1959   227
Malaria Eradication, June, 1959   228

Foreword

THE EXPLOSIVE FERMENT that culminated in Asia's social and political revolution was epitomized in the struggle for independence in Vietnam. Interestingly, few occurrences in recent years seem to have been attended by as much publicity—and misinformation—as those which took place when French rule in Southeast Asia came to an end and independent entities were established in its stead. Over the latter years of French dominion the world was offered a continuing stream of news stories and official releases which tended to develop an inaccurate and confused picture of developments in Indochina: France was defending the honor and civilization of the West against barbarian Communist hordes; freedom in Vietnam could best be defended by Frenchmen fighting against the people of Vietnam; the war against Communism in Vietnam was nearly won; the Vietnamese did not really want to be separated from France, their benefactor and protector; in the last analysis, the Vietnamese were really children, and were incapable of governing themselves.

After eight years of civil war in the Southeast Asian peninsula, France finally sat down at Geneva in April 1954, with the Communist leaders of the Vietnamese rebellion, the non-Communist representatives of the French-sponsored State of Vietnam, and the foreign ministers of the world's great and interested powers. In the midst of the Geneva Conference, the great French fortress of Dien Bien Phu, in northwest Vietnam, fell to the rebel armies, and with this dramatic event fell also France's hopes of salvaging some part of her Asian holdings. Simultaneously, the curtain of propaganda which for years had masked the true character of things in Vietnam also fell away, and the world at large saw for the first time the complex and depressing situation that existed there. When the conferees decided upon a horizontal partition of Vietnam, the most optimistic estimate heard in the corridors of Geneva was that the southern segment, which had been awarded to the French-sponsored regime of Bao Dai, might last as long as two years before formally joining its northern half under Communist rule. The chaotic conditions which obviously prevailed in the south were considered impossible of successful resolution by its non-Communist leaders. And most of the

v

world sat back to await the inevitable ending. The appearance of the present volume is ample testimony to the fact that the "inescapable" did not occur. On October 26, 1961, the Republic of Vietnam—organized the result of a chain of events that led from the disaster of Geneva in July of 1954 to the termination of the French-linked Vietnamese monarchy by a popular referendum—celebrated its sixth anniversary.

It is sometimes difficult even for those of us who knew Vietnam at the time of the Geneva Conference to comprehend fully the progress of these few years. By the same token, we sometimes tend to exaggerate the depth of the changes which have occurred and to misinterpret their essential character. Friends and critics alike are often inclined to forget the chaos that was Vietnam in July 1954, and to measure the nature and extent of change there against an irrelevant and misleading model—a present-day American yardstick.

In appraising the character of developments in the Republic of Vietnam, the analyst finds himself juggling a bushel of balls. The variables seem to be myriad, given the country's physical location and neighbors, its traditions and historical development, its economic, political, military, and social problems, its needs, and its ambitions. In the analytic process, one finds himself shifting back and forth, from a tendency to search through a mass of frequently contradictory data for a "simple solution," to a proclivity to succumb to the apparently hopeless complexity of the situation. The student of Vietnamese affairs has suffered also from a plethora of conflicting data in some areas, and from a frustrating scarcity of reliable information in others.

It was with the hope of shedding illumination on various aspects of the process and problems of development in Free Vietnam that the American Friends of Vietnam, a non-partisan organization formed in 1955 to foster goodwill and understanding between the people of the United States and Vietnam, sponsored a Conference on Social Development and Welfare in the young Republic.

In opening the sessions, Lt. Gen. John W. O'Daniel, USA (Ret.), National Chairman of the American Friends of Vietnam, observed that "the high sounding generalities of the independence struggle gain their true significance by the degree to which the government of a newly independent nation can succeed in realizing progress in these areas for the majority of the people."

Held at the Roosevelt Hotel in New York City on October 23 and 24, 1959, the Conference was attended by more than 200 scholars, businessmen, government officials, and journalists. Twenty-nine scholars and specialists, representing a major portion of the authoritative knowledge in the United States on Vietnamese affairs, presented papers or commentaries at the two-day meeting. The present volume consists of revised, updated, and enlarged versions of most of those papers. The essay by Joseph Buttinger was not delivered at the Conference for lack of time, and John C. Donnell, whose essay is also included, was not able to attend the meetings.

As Conference Chairman, I wish to express my gratitude to the members of the Conference Planning Committee: Joseph Buttinger, Leo Cherne, David Cole, Rev. Francis J. Corley, S. J., John T. Dorsey, Jr., Milton Esman, Roy Jumper, Wolf Ladejinsky, Richard W. Lindholm, Walter W. Mode, Robert R. Nathan, Guy J. Pauker, Milton Sacks, and Stanley K. Sheinbaum. Their advice and guidance were invaluable. Appreciation is also due to Ambassador G. Frederick Reinhardt (then Counselor of the U. S. Department of State) and to Ambassador Tran Van Chuong of the Republic of Vietnam for their stimulating addresses; to Joseph Buttinger, James Fesler, J. Lossing Buck, and Kenneth T. Young, for chairing the working sessions of the Conference; to the participating scholars and specialists for the hard work and consummate skill that went into the preparation of their papers; and to Hilda Jaffe for her conscientious cooperation in preparing the manuscript for publication. Finally, the authors of this volume are indebted to the New Lands Foundation for its encouragement and support of this enterprise.

Wesley R. Fishel

East Lansing, Michigan
August, 1961

Introduction

I RECALL VIVIDLY conversations with Ngo Dinh Diem six years ago this month in Saigon, a few weeks after he had become Vietnam's new premier. He drew a picture of a situation that was unbelievably grave. Intrigue, plots, threats, insurrection—these were commonplace in Vietnam late in 1954 when we talked, a situation which was to persist through most of 1955.

During those unpredictable days, almost the only thread that linked the multiplicity of forces in Vietnam was their general agreement that Ngo Dinh Diem must go. The array of opposition seemed to include every segment of power in the newly-independent nation—the quasi-religious sects and the bandit-pirate combines with their private armies, political cliques within and outside the Government, foreign circles, Communist cadres who had not departed for the North, and even parts of the National Army itself. Poised on the 17th parallel was the battle-hardened army of the Viet Minh. Western journalists and political leaders almost unanimously chorused prophesies of prompt doom for the new government of Ngo Dinh Diem. On every score the odds against his survival seemed insurmountable.

The one factor not fully considered in this political equation was the Vietnamese people in the beleaguered, war-weary South. In those critical months when Vietnam's fate hung in the balance, very few correctly analyzed the role of the people. The significant exceptions, as recent history must now acknowledge, were Ngo Dinh Diem and his colleagues. They sensed fully that a legitimate nationalist government concerned with popular welfare could rally the nation behind a unified national effort. Where many predicted that the Army would not stand up and fight, the new Premier issued the battle call and the Army fought—and fought well. One by one the dissident groups fell, the disloyal elements in the Army were expelled, the foreign threats receded, the people rallied to the new sense of nationhood.

A year later, in the autumn of 1955, I again visited Vietnam. Already the change was remarkable. What had seemed to be a nightmare of chaos one year earlier was then shaping into a solid, hopeful situation. I was able to write in a report to the Foreign Relations Committee on October 6, 1955, that

> The tide of totalitarian communism has slackened. A year ago it was
> on the verge of overrunning the entire country and much of the rest
> of Southeast Asia. That threat has now been reduced. There is today
> a reasonable chance of the survival and development of a free Vietnam.
> It should be emphasized, however, that what has been gained during
> the past year is a chance not a guarantee. It has been gained largely
> through the dedication and courage of Ngo Dinh Diem.

To many Americans the mere achievement of survival is itself an
extraordinary achievement for the Free Vietnamese. I must say can-
didly, however, that political survival is in itself nothing more than a
relative accomplishment. If Free Vietnam's sole achievement had been
political survival, I would today be far less hopeful about that Southeast Asian ally.

In retrospect one can discern three rather clearly defined stages in
South Vietnam's development since the division of that country at
Geneva in July, 1954. Until mid-1956, the principal goal was to weld
a unified nation by absorbing or eliminating the dissident forces. The
next two years saw a process of consolidation, the most important
aspect of which was the successful integration of hundreds of thousands of refugees from the Communist zone. A new constitution was
promulgated, following Vietnam's first national election for a Con-
stituent Assembly. The form of a representative system was established
and the Republic of Vietnam launched. Between the form and the
practice of representative democracy, there was—and there is likely
to be—considerable divergence for some time to come, as Wesley
Fishel demonstrates in his chapter on the problems of political development. The direction, however, has been established.

During this period of consolidation, a new and modern Vietnamese
National Army was built and trained to assume the tasks of internal
security and national defense. In every significant test the Army proved
loyal to the Government, a fact that cannot be lightly ignored. Vice
was crushed and corruption in Government sharply reduced from what
had existed before the advent of the Republican government. The
enormous task began of clearing overgrown ricelands, cleaning irrigation ditches and canals, repairing dikes, and rebuilding all that had
been destroyed or laid waste in a generation of civil war.

Thus it was that in late 1957 the Vietnamese republic embarked on
the third, and most important, phase of its upward climb. It not only
faced the job of rebuilding what had been shattered by war; it was
now confronted with the even more formidable undertaking of building
a new society, of modernizing to provide a higher living standard to all
of its people, of eliminating the injustices and imbalances it inherited

from the old order. The papers recorded in this volume are the docu-
mented account of Vietnam's real revolution. Here are the evidences
of important strides toward fulfilling the aspirations of the common
people. In Chapter 10, for example, Wolf Ladejinsky describes the
scope of Free Asia's second largest land reform program, which includes both redistribution with compensation and tenant security. In
Mr. Tran Ngoc Lien's chapter there is reported the growth of a progressive agricultural credit program, to be followed by a broad and
penetrating cooperative movement so that the people may share more
fully in the fruits of their labor. Sections on health, education, and
labor indicate that a better life is taking root in Vietnam. These
changes are the implicit promises of national independence in Asia
today and their fulfillment is essential to Asian stability.

There is another theme which echoes throughout the scholarly
analyses contained in this volume—that is a pioneering spirit which
seems to characterize the Vietnamese. The Vietnamese display a
propensity for striking out in new realms with untried methods and
techniques heretofore unknown to their country. They display a high
degree of flexibility and imagination. The manner in which they im-
provised the resettlement of their refugee brothers from the North is
one example. The huge Cai San agricultural development project in
the Mekong delta is another. And the most dramatic is, of course, the
"Westward Ho" movement into the high plateau, where to date more
than one hundred thousand Vietnamese, traditionally wedded to
coastal lowland rice-farming, have taken up a new life and grow new
crops in new surroundings. William Henderson, in Chapter 7, provides
the first full account of this remarkable transformation. The highlands
development symbolizes in a tangible way Vietnam's recent growth,
telescoping decades into years, substituting airplanes and tractors for
covered wagons and bullock-drawn plows, but getting the job done.

There are a few brushstrokes in the picture presented by this book
which, I feel, need further emphasis. The role of American support
is by and large hinted at, rather than articulated, and this is appropriate, for the book deals with Vietnam's own social development and
welfare. But through Mutual Security and other forms of aid the
Vietnamese were accorded that extra and vital ingredient without
which their determination and energy could not have accomplished
all that has been done to date. Several hundred Americans, backed
by almost $2 billion in commodities and equipment, have assisted the
Vietnamese in building their army, consolidating their fiscal and administrative independence, expanding health, credit, agricultural and

educational services to the people, and, in recent months, in building new industry. America diplomatic support did much to enable the Free Vietnamese Government to resist otherwise calamitous pressures. Let us not mistake this point: the primary responsibility for the achievements in Vietnam rests with the Vietnamese people and their leaders. American aid could never have substituted for their inspiration, hard work, and dedication, but the two have proved a fortunate combination, with the American people helping another people to help itself in freedom.

In late 1959 I headed a subcommittee of the Foreign Relations Committee which, among other things, reviewed the course of aid administration in Vietnam. I was especially struck by the real evidence of Vietnam's ability to help itself. My colleagues were equally impressed with the initiative demonstrated by the Vietnamese in shaping and carrying out their own programs. The land development and railroad reconstruction programs are but two examples from which lessons may be learned in our approach to aid administration. As our report noted, these two programs, originated by the Vietnamese despite certain misgivings on the part of aid administrators, proved highly successful, so much so that they are now pointed to as major achievements of the aid program. They suggest that more consideration must be given in the future to activities in which the content of Vietnamese initiative is high.

There has been waste in our aid program in Vietnam, as elsewhere, but there has also been great achievement in Vietnam, and that should not be overlooked in any evaluation of the effort. For those who question the value of the aid program in helping to provide a better, more decent life in Vietnam a careful reading of this volume ought to dispel most doubts.

The job in Vietnam is not completed. The scope of Vietnam's economic and social problems is such that all the achievements to date comprise little more than a good start. No one realizes this better than the Vietnamese leaders themselves. The struggle to rebuild what was destroyed was, in a major sense, far easier than the future struggle to create a modern society will be. This will require industrial and other developments, in itself a tremendous undertaking, but even more so since Free Vietnam must simultaneously bear the burden of a continuing war of terror and subversion.

Yet without significant development, higher living standards and internal stability in freedom cannot be achieved and Vietnam cannot become economically self-supporting. With wise assistance, however, there is every reason to believe that Vietnam can achieve adequate development and self-support without resort to totalitarian methods.

Ultimately Vietnam's future lies with its neighbors in South and Southeast Asia. The real job must be done by the Asians themselves. This is no less true of economic and social advance than it is of military defense. This means that the first line of defense must be the peoples of each Asian nation. It also means that they may ultimately respond collectively with an Asian system of security.

A common approach to the problems of hunger, poverty and disease is equally imperative for the free nations of Asia. Their resources are too limited to allow for duplication of effort. The growth of a regional consciousness, followed by a regional attack on mutual problems, can in the end contribute more to their progress than any bilateral or solo undertakings. President Ngo Dinh Diem has been among the foremost spokesmen for such an approach. In September, 1959 he called for the creation of a common market for Southeast Asia as a means of speeding up industrial development without resorting to the Communist method and as a way to obtaining better terms of trade for the raw materials of the region which are exchanged for machinery. "It seems to me," he concluded, "that it is on this basis that the countries of Southeast Asia could group themselves solidly to defend their interests and to share with one another their experiences. I am firmly convinced of the feasibility of accomplishing this."

Within Vietnam, the problems of industrialization and modernization are obstructed in large measure by the shortage of trained personnel— technicians, teachers and, above all, administrators and managers, both governmental and private. This is unquestionably a product of Vietnam's history, but it constitutes the principal roadblock to extensive action on the Government's plans and policies. Professor Dorsey, in Chapter 8, deals sensitively with the administrative problems of an Asian society in transition. These problems, more than any other, deserve the most thoughtful study as well as the most imaginative assistance. Vietnam's labor force, both in terms of its skill and its ability to organize freely, is dealt with effectively by Professor Hendry. These questions of productivity and economic justice are especially compelling to Asia's eventual freedom. Our understanding of their implications is barely beyond the threshold.

These, then, are some of the outlines of Vietnam's future problems in achieving a just, plentiful and free society. Americans can hope for nothing more worthwhile than their solution, for the ends of freedom and a stable peace are equally served by their attainment. We can count on the determination of the Vietnamese. This we have learned from the past five years. I believe they can count equally on American support to carry through their measures of reform and building. The job ahead is most difficult. But in view of what Free Vietnam has achieved to date there is reason to hope that it will be done.

Mike Mansfield
United States Senate
July 30, 1960

PROBLEMS OF FREEDOM

South Vietnam
Since Independence

CHAPTER 1

The Consequences of Partition

*by Robert R. Nathan**

THE PARTITION of Vietnam in 1954 climaxed the almost unbelievable sequence of disrupting and destructive events that had befallen the nation ever since the beginning of World War II.

Under several generations of French colonial domination, the economic development of Indochina had been largely directed toward French political and economic objectives, and not at all toward the realization of the nation's maximum economic potential. The Japanese occupation during World War II halted even this limited rate of development and was followed by widespread destruction. After the war, the denial of legitimate nationalist aspirations was seized upon by the Communists as an excuse for insurrection and subversion. Major hostilities tore the country apart and produced economic chaos. The partition of Vietnam in 1954 left the Communists in control of the north, while the Republic of Vietnam achieved independence in the south. Real peace, however, continues to be an elusive aspiration for the people of Vietnam.

Since then the relations with Laos and Cambodia—the rest of what had been French Indochina—have suffered from many economic disturbances. Trade and investment relations with France have changed very greatly, and there is nothing approaching either political or economic normalcy in the area formerly under the dominion of France.

As a result of this recent chaotic history, the direct consequences of the partition itself are extremely difficult to separate from the effects of war and insurrection and the change from colonial status. Nor would such an analysis have more than limited significance even if it could be made. The complexity of Vietnam's situation and the diverse influences affecting its development are such as to make Korea, for example, seem relatively uncomplicated.

*Robert R. Nathan is president of Robert R. Nathan Associates, Inc., Economic Consultants, formerly advisor to the Embassy of Vietnam in Washington, D. C.

1

It is both useful and revealing to compare the economic characteristics of pre-partition Vietnam with those of the southern sector now comprising the Republic of Vietnam. However, additional factors must be recognized if one is to gain a full understanding of the problems the Republic must solve before it can achieve economic viability. The newly-won independence must be consolidated and civil government stabilized; wartime destruction must be repaired; a continued high level of outlay for defense must be provided for; internal and external threats to security must be controlled; population shifts must be directed; and many other problems solved.

The effect of partition on a reasonably balanced economy was the creation of distortions and dislocations that cannot be remedied overnight. No country is truly self-sufficient, since all carry on some foreign trade. Nevertheless, patterns develop in each nation that tend to maximize internal trade and minimize external trade. This is not to imply a general tendency toward self-sufficiency, but a country's patterns of internal resource-use and production tend toward an integrated and complementary set of economic relationships and correspondingly less external trade than might be expected in the absence of political boundaries.

When a nation is partitioned, and trade is cut off between areas where it flowed freely before, costly readjustments will inevitably be needed. While the loss of a small area might be sustained without adverse effects, the removal of half a nation's territory is bound to result in severe economic dislocation. The consequences of partition are especially disruptive when there is wide variation in production structure. Economic and industrial development seldom proceeds uniformly throughout a nation, since it reflects geographical variation and differs according to available resources. Indochina naturally showed such variation, and its economic structure had a resulting lack of homogeneity.

Before World War II the resources and output of the three regions that comprised Vietnam before partition—Cochinchina in the south, Tonkin in the north, and Annam in the middle—largely complemented each other. The north was more heavily industrial, while the central and southern regions were mainly agricultural.

South Vietnam (Cochinchina), one of the great rice-surplus areas of the world, had some light industry, but was largely agricultural. Besides rice it produced rubber, corn, sugar, peanuts, copra, tobacco, tea, coffee, sweet potatoes, jute, kapok, and a variety of other crops. Industrial activity was concentrated in the Saigon area and principally included agricultural processing, especially rice milling; light consumer industries such as the making of beer, soft drinks, soap, matches, ice, salt, cigarettes, etc.; some chemical production (oxygen, carbonic gas. and acetylene); and the generation of electricity from coal.

Central Vietnam (Annam) produced some rice, corn, and other agricultural commodities, raised cattle, mined gold and other minerals, and engaged in some light industry. Northern Vietnam (Tonkin) was devoted mainly to agriculture, mining, and manufacturing. It employed many thousands of workers in textile, paper, chemical, glass, cement, and fertilizer factories.

The southern half of Vietnam provided the north with rice—as much as a half million tons a year—and also exported large quantities to other countries. It shipped to the north cotton, corn, copra and many other farm products, as well as dried, salted fish from its coastal waters and rivers. The northern half of Vietnam, with its preponderance of natural resources and industrial capacity, produced many of the manufactured goods and raw materials consumed by the south.

As a result of the Geneva Agreements of July 20, 1954, which brought to an end the eight-year-old war and partitioned Vietnam at approximately the 17th parallel, the Republic of Vietnam lost the rich and productive resources and the markets of half of Annam and all of Tonkin, an area of over 60,000 square miles and containing then approximately 14 million persons.

The loss of large supplies of coal from the north was perhaps the most serious immediate consequence of partition. While the Republic of Vietnam does have coal, it had been more economic to exploit the north's large reserve of high-quality anthracite which, before the war, had supplied the country's requirements in full. Nearly all of South Vietnam's electricity production depended on coal from the north.

Of great significance, especially, was the concentration of the textile industry in the north. The cotton gins and spinning and weaving mills were in the north, and produced enough yarn and cloth to supply half of the country's requirements.

The north supplied in full all of Vietnam's cement: before the war the cement plant at Haiphong, near Hanoi, produced more than 300 thousand tons a year and, after supplying the needs of the country, had 75 thousand tons left for export.

The north's high-grade deposits of apatite (a source of phosphorus) and its crushing facilities took care of all of Vietnam's pre-war needs for phosphate fertilizers. It supplied as well limestone, chemicals, glass, paper, and other industrial products consumed by the south.

The loss of these industrial resources and facilities consequently made a restructuring of the south's economy necessary. However, in the process distortions were created by the necessity of locating new facilities according to defensive or politically strategic reasons, and by the concentration of labor surpluses in less productive sectors of the economy. The cost-price structure was further distorted by the need to obtain and distribute quickly supplies that had formerly been purchased, relatively inexpensively, from the north. The large commercial import program, maintained to provide the Vietnamese Government with local currency under the United States foreign aid program, further contributed to the difficulties.

Another major problem was the need to find new markets for surplus products. When commerce across the 17th parallel terminated, new outlets had to be found for southern products previously shipped to the north. For a time, the presence of French military forces provided a vast market for local goods and services, but their withdrawal after partition compounded the south's difficulties.

Fiscal and monetary consequences following partition were the need for deficit financing of military operations, transfer of bank deposits from north to south, etc., though with implications different from the dislocations in resources and markets.

The economic impact of these changes arising out of partition was magnified by the extent to which World War II and the Communist insurrection had disabled the economy of the south. Roads, railroads, and inland waterways were severely damaged, creating serious bottlenecks in the movement of goods and people, and ships and smaller watercraft were demolished. The mere rehabilitation of what had been destroyed, dismantled, or otherwise put out of commission was itself a heavy burden on the economy.

Even in agriculture, the impact of years of war and internal disorder was staggering, leading to abandonment of more than a million acres of paddy land in the southern half of Vietnam. Paddy lands cannot be left idle for long without deterioration of irrigation canals and dikes from salt water seepage, jungle growth, and the like. The restoration of such lands is costly and time-consuming. Further, there was much loss of livestock, and exports of rice, Vietnam's most important foreign-exchange earner, fell from a half million tons a year to a small fraction of this total.

The situation in rubber, second in importance in Vietnam's foreign exchange earnings, was comparable. The prolonged guerilla warfare severely reduced production. Other chops like copra and corn, significant though relatively less important to foreign exchange earnings, were reduced to a mere trickle. Fishery production, too, fell sharply and fish exports practically disappeared.

Another immediate development with an adverse economic impact was the departure of many French firms and businessmen with their technicians, managers and, sometimes, their equipment. No colonial power truly develops the maximum skills and capabilities of a subjected people. This was certainly true in Vietnam, where most of the positions of top responsibility and authority in economic affairs were in the hands of the French. Independence was followed by an exodus of many French enterprises and skilled personnel, an intensive repatriation of capital, and an almost complete stoppage of new French investment.

The loss of skills and experiences was particularly serious. There are no data on occupational characteristics of the people of Vietnam immediately before partition, but pre-World War II figures on the regional distribution of artisans and industrial workers are available. In 1937, there were over 95,000 artisans in Tonkin in the north as compared with under 20,000 in Cochinchina in the south and under 13,000 in Annam in the central section of the country. The presence of nearly 57,000 artisans in textile industries in Tonkin in 1937, as compared with only some 3,000 in Annam and just a few hundred in Cochinchina, is especially significant. Only in woodworking was there a large number of artisans in Cochinchina (over 4,000) and Annam (about 2,800). In papermaking there were nearly 2,800 artisans in the north, but just a handful in the central and southern parts of the country. Tonkin had more than 40,000 workers in important mining companies before World War II, whereas estimates indicate no significant number of industrial workers in mining in the south. Similarly, most of the industrial workers in important manufacturing plants were in Tonkin.

Since the federal capital was in Hanoi, along with most of the head offices of large firms and the University, the major portion of the country's professional and administrative personnel were concentrated in the north. The key to economic development lies in the experience and training of workers and management, and the loss of skills and experience resulting from partition was a significant disadvantage to the Republic of Vietnam.

The movement of large numbers of refugees into South Vietnam brought with it a number of serious economic problems. While the influx of refugees did add to manpower availability, being a source of skills and talents which has already increased the level of production and should continue to do so, the problems of large-scale immigration were an added burden on South Vietnam's economy. The unemployment problem was aggravated, and transportation, housing, and health facilities were severely taxed. The immediate needs of the refugees for food, shelter, and clothing were, of course, only the first of their requirements. Public facilities—water, schools, roads, power, and the like—had to be provided, and the immigrants somehow absorbed into the economy. Capital formation was required to increase the nation's economic productivity. The burden of the current maintenance of the refugees, plus the problem of their ultimate economic absorption, has added to the already serious economic situation in South Vietnam.

The continued insecurity—the ever-present threat of invasion from North Vietnam and of subversion from within—has made it imperative to maintain a large military establishment which has been very costly to the economy. Able young men have had to be diverted from more productive endeavors. Goods and services produced by the civilian population have had to be diverted to the army. Military expenditures inject buying power into the economy which poses a serious inflationary threat. While military training does develop a number of skills, and some defense forces produce basic facilities helpful to the economy, in the aggregate South Vietnam's defense effort has imposed a major burden on the economy of the country. This, too, is a direct consequence of partition.

The total impact of all these results of partition is so great that one can only admire a nation which has been able to survive under such difficulties. It is against this background that one must evaluate the Republic of Vietnam's progress to date and its need for cooperation and assistance from the free world if it is to consolidate these achievements and lay a foundation for a sound, self-supporting economy.

Because of the impact of partition and the other adverse forces described above, the economic development program for the Republic of Vietnam must vary considerably from those of other less developed or less war-torn nations. Clearly the economic task is not merely one of rebuilding what was destroyed by hostilities and then pursuing a reasonably normal process of economic expansion. The future economic pattern of the area now occupied by the Republic of Vietnam must differ basically from the economic pattern of that same geographic area prior to partition. The important changes in sources of supplies and in markets will necessitate major differences.

The achievement of independence has made important changes from past economic patterns necessary. The end of French colonialism brought problems of encouraging new foreign investors, stimulating the expansion of the entrepreneurial class, broadening export markets (with less reliance on the franc area), and generally adapting the trade pattern so that imports and exports would relate to each other in a manner consistent with a sound balance of payments, both in magnitude and in composition.

The pattern of development will also deviate considerably from that before partition because of technological changes. A highly industrialized economy cannot be evolved over-night, and it is therefore essential that in agriculture, forestry, transportation, industry and other activities, the Republic of Vietnam take the fullest possible advantage of new techniques and new processes for stepping up productivity and production.

The economic programming task is made especially complex by the inflationary pressures resulting from the huge defense program and the development effort. Financing a large defense program without inflation is always difficult. To undertake at the same time a large investment program presents inflationary threats which require careful and thorough financial programming designed to mobilize internal savings as well as foreign private and public capital to the greatest possible extent.

In view of the magnitude of the task, and the severity and complexity of the obstacles, the Republic of Vietnam must continue to depend substantially on foreign assistance for some years to come. The immediate task is to program development so as to reduce this reliance on foreign aid gradually. The pressures resulting from defense and investment outlays bring the danger that inflation can be held in check only by an ever-increasing inflow of consumer goods and a large and growing trade deficit. It can be minimized only by sound internal fiscal policies that will generate more and more internal savings as the economy expands. Policies must be developed which strike a proper balance between providing the necessary financial resources for government investment and minimum interference with incentives for private investment.

Unfortunately, the consequences of partition outlined above have not by any means been dissipated. The Republic of Vietnam will have to bear the burden of them for some years to come. It cannot bear these burdens alone. The gain to the free world more than justifies the maximum of assistance in providing the means for building in the Republic of Vietnam a sound, viable, and dynamic economy which can serve as an example of what a determined free people can accomplish.

Despite all the disadvantages and difficulties, the Republic of Vietnam does have the potential for excellent economic progress. While the country is blessed with a favorable supply of good land and other natural resources, its greatest asset is its people. They are hard-working and capable, and have demonstrated their determination and their capacity to suffer and to fight for their ideals, and for freedom and independence.

Given the capital and technical assistance so necessary to economic development, I am confident that the people of South Vietnam will prove that they can overcome their present problems and stand as a free nation.

CHAPTER 2

Problems of Democratic Growth in Free Vietnam

by Wesley R. Fishel*

VIETNAM ACHIEVED its independence after a long and painful campaign of opposition to the French colonial regime. The attainment of independence in 1954 did not, however, bring with it any sweeping away of the colonial heritage. Ninety years of occupation by a group of alien rulers had left marks unlikely ever to be completely eliminated. Coming with advanced techniques, the French wrought great changes in the traditional patterns of Vietnamese society, and in the course of subordinating the Vietnamese people to the ends of the colonial power they disrupted and inevitably altered the native culture and drastically modified its moral and ethical values. The resultant society was a product of political miscegenation: one with a traditional base, influenced by Confucian, Taoist, and Buddhist ideas and values, topped by a weighty superstructure of Western organizations, principles, laws, and techniques.

Saigon was occupied by French forces in 1860, and in 1867 South Vietnam (then called Cochinchina) became a colony of France, governed directly, in the same fashion as Algeria. Pursuing the time-honored principle of "Divide and Conquer," the French encouraged regional separatism by splitting the country into three different regimes. South Vietnam (Cochinchina) was a true colony; Central Vietnam (Annam) and North Vietnam (Tonkin) were made protectorates. These three administrative units were then joined with the kingdoms of Laos and Cambodia to form an Indochinese Federation. During World War II, Admiral Decoux, then Governor General of Indochina, gave further encouragement to local "patriotism," and in 1946 his successor, Admiral d'Argenlieu, sponsored the establishment of the "Republic of Cochinchina."

*Dr. Wesley R. Fishel is Professor of Political Science at Michigan State University, and was Chief Advisor of the Michigan State University Advisory Group in Vietnam, 1956-1958. He also served in Vietnam in 1954-1955 as Consultant on Governmental Reorganization to the U. S. Operations Mission.

9

The French brought to Vietnam their own administrative system and their own economic concepts and objectives. The traditional autonomy of the villages was taken away; the old patterns of land distribution and tenure were altered; in the north large estates were secured by acquisitive landowners through usurious credit practices. Using the Annamese monarchy as their tool, the French expertly manipulated the mandarinate to consolidate their control over the people at the local levels of government. And the corruption, debasement, and debilitation of the Vietnamese was expedited by the colonial regime's efficient monopolistic control of the production and distribution of alcohol and opium. It is true that through extensive programs of public works, health, and sanitation, the French facilitated communication between various areas of the country, irrigated hundreds of thousands of acres of farm land, introduced new crops, and improved health conditions in the cities. At the same time, one must also grant some validity to the Vietnamese claim that these measures benefited the Vietnamese only indirectly, having been initiated primarily to increase the exploitative potential of the colony and mitigate the hardships of life there for the colonists. With all that the French accomplished in Vietnam, at the time of the Geneva Conference of 1954 the country remained underdeveloped and fundamentally agricultural; its administration, production, and exportation were correlated to the needs of the French rather than to those of the Vietnamese.

In Vietnam, as in most colonial countries, the leadership of nationalist political groups during the colonial period often came from the more westernized professional and intellectual groups: from the students, the lawyers, the doctors; in other words, from people who had been exposed more or less directly to western influences and ideas, and had drawn from their studies the heady and dangerous ideas of freedom and human rights. With a few exceptions, relatively few of the pre-independence nationalists came from the ranks of the bureaucracy. For the bureaucracy was the creation and instrument of the colonial administration, and by and large it tended to attract the seeker after security and power, rather than the agitator and revolutionary. Many of the early leaders came from well-to-do families, or from families of traditional political influence. In general, these nationalists thought and acted in a framework of intrigue and secrecy aimed toward the overthrow of the colonial regime. But rarely did their planning encompass the less immediate, but far more complicated and important problems that would have to be solved once independence was achieved.

II

When in July, 1954, the Conference of Geneva partitioned Vietnam into two halves—Communist and non-Communist—the colonial division of the country into three regions was brought to an end. True, the administrative form itself was retained in the non-Communist zone, south of the 17th parallel. But with the avalanche of northern refugees who descended on the south during the next 300 days a new epoch of amalgamation and integration began. The influx of northerners created friction in the countryside and in the towns as well. Nearly 300 new villages were created in the course of refugee resettlement. Towns became overcrowded, the population of the Saigon-Cholon metropolitan area increased sharply, and the southerners, accustomed to an easy, relaxed way of life, found in their midst some 850,000 aggressive, energetic, hard-working countrymen from north of the 17th parallel who spoke their language, but with a pronunciation not always easy to understand. The misunderstandings and friction normal to such circumstances were intensified by subtle Communist propaganda, as well as by the general uncertainty and uneasiness current at that time that gave every rumor, no matter how wild, the standing of a sacred text.

As the months have passed, however, there have been heartening signs that the fear, suspicion, and antagonisms that marked these initial contacts between the refugees and the original southerners are lessening. Although the northerners tended to move south in village units, and tried to establish themselves once more in separate villages, the artificial barriers between them and their southern neighbors are breaking down. For one thing, the language is becoming standardized. Some northerners have moved from their new villages to towns where they are more easily merged with the southerners. Too, there has been an increasing number of marriages between young people of the two groups. Finally, as the southerners have come to understand the sacrifices made by their new neighbors, and have heard repeatedly the tales of what they were subjected to in the North, there has resulted a growing general appreciation of the Communist danger.

Although it did not immediately disturb the regional divisions of its territory established by the French, the new Vietnamese government, headed by Prime Minister Ngo Dinh Diem, saw from the outset that its chances of survival were slight unless it could stimulate a rapid development of national consciousness and engender strong popular support. The Vietnamese peasant—88 per cent of the Republic's population is rural—has traditionally been loyal to his family and to his village, not his nation. So far the effects of European contact have mainly been shown in the growing use of relatively non-essential Western objects such as cotton or silk print garments, hats, umbrellas, and cigarette lighters. In the fields the peasant still uses the same kind of plough his great-grandfather used. His vision focuses on his village, and it is only on special occasions that he has been accustomed to travel far beyond its limits. This parochial outlook is not confined to the peasantry: most of the high-ranking members of the national civil service have never been outside Vietnam, and many of the ordinary civil servants have never even been to the nation's capital.

With orientations and horizons so generally limited, the task before the new regime was remarkably difficult. If one takes into account also the extraordinary political confusion—the jockeying for position of ambitious politicians and generals, the maneuvers of the Hoa Hao, Cao Dai, and Binh Xuyen leaders, the intrigues of Bao Dai and his retinue of courtiers and counselors, and the schemes of the French—the dimensions of the problem were staggering.

It is not the province of this paper to recapitulate the events of 1954-1956. They have been told many times. However, it is relevant to trace briefly some of the shifts occurring in the political realm during this period.

The elimination of French authority left a sudden, and nearly disastrous, political vacuum. True, there was a new government, headed by a most respected nationalist. It was also true that there was no lack of patriots on whom Prime Minister Ngo Dinh Diem could call for assistance. What was lacking, however, was experienced administrators. As in many colonial countries, Vietnam had only a thin veneer of managerial expertise that remained when the French withdrew. One might well assert that the most important problem in Vietnamese administration has been the grave shortage of trained and competent technicians and administrators. As all administrators and many politicians are aware, it takes more than patriotism and good will to keep a governmental machine in operation. Ngo Dinh Diem's first cabinet was staffed with loyal men, most of whom were completely new to administrative routines. Further, the existing bureaucratic personnel had entered their profession under French auspices, and their duties had been, in the main, to carry out French decisions rather than to make decisions themselves. Oriented toward the former colonial regime by virtue of their training and their appointments, and, like the majority of their countrymen, not then convinced that the new nationalist government would long survive, many of the bureaucracy dragged their feet, or, in some instances, simply ignored, or pigeon-holed, orders from the new ministers. The result was a partial paralysis of the administrative mechanism lasting for several weeks.

The two politico-religious sects, the Cao Dai and the Hoa Hao, who, with armies totaling 50,000 men, held sway in feudal fashion over extensive fiefs which the French had granted them in South Vietnam, occupied their time in a sort of continuing assessment of their own (and everyone else's) chances of gaining power. Similarly, the Binh Xuyen, controlling the police, gambling, prostitution, and the narcotics traffic in the capital area and boasting a well-trained and equipped force of some 5,000 soldiers, met first with one group and then another, forming alliances that lasted a few days or weeks and were in turn succeeded by other alliances. The leadership of the National Army, under Gen. Nguyen Van Hinh, son of former Prime Minister Nguyen Van Tam and himself an officer in the French Air Force, was also deeply involved in a bewildering succession of secret meetings and plots whose general purpose was to decide who should constitute the government which would follow the inevitable and early fall of the Ngo Dinh Diem regime.

These moves (and counter-moves by the Government itself) went on beneath the surface, reaching a sub-climax on September 24, 1954, when the Prime Minister adroitly maneuvered the leaders of the Cao Dai and Hoa Hao into his revamped cabinet as a device for gaining time. Then, during the following spring, the final crisis occurred when the Binh Xuyen, despairing of a successful alternative solution, opened fire on the Presidential Palace in Saigon, and civil warfare broke out. These developments were accompanied by a number of surface manifestations which, while not as substantively significant, throw light on the problem of democratic growth in this country.

As the reality of independence sank into the consciousness of politically alert Vietnamese, they came to realize that, while they might count on the French either for further occasional help, or as still capable and influential malefactors,[1] the United States was now exerting the greatest amount of influence on political events in Vietnam. There was, consequently, a burst of democratic and pseudo-democratic ideas and propaganda across the entire Vietnamese political horizon. Pious democratic credos were uttered by men who had till then been considered power-hungry political scoundrels. Groups of opposition politicians who were known to have teamed up with authoritarian Hoa Hao or Cao Dai generals sought out Americans and essayed more or less convincing preachments on their attachment to the democratic cause. The glamour-touched and persuasive idea of a "government of national unity" with its "roots among the people" was pushed ardently by politicians and feudal barons of all stripes. As we look back now, we can see that all of this was quite insignificant. None of these articulate men has come to power. The power of the two sects and of the Binh Xuyen has been broken. The Army has been demonstrably loyal to the Government.[2]

III

In passing to a consideration of the problems facing the present government and the steps it is taking to solve them, it is useful to pause briefly for a sketch of the background of political development in Vietnam. One ought not to use the term "political parties" in speaking of developments in Vietnam unless he interprets that term rather broadly. During the ninety years of French domination in the Indochinese peninsula, political organizations of all kinds were outlawed until, at the close of the Second World War, the French granted the Vietnamese a degree of autonomy and thereby fostered the establishment of a quasi-autonomous regime, permitting at the same time the more or less open activity of such auxiliary paraphernalia as political parties.

This is not to say that political organizations did not exist prior to the restoration of Bao Dai in 1949. Certainly the activities of the Communists and of numerous non-Communist nationalist alliances were political. However, though they called themselves "parties," they were, more accurately, "secret societies" organized to promote particular political programs. In nearly every case their ultimate objectives were the overthrow of French rule and their own accession to power.

For example, the *Viet Nam Duy Tan Hoi* [Association for the Modernization of Vietnam] was founded shortly after the beginning of the twentieth century with the purpose of developing an anti-French revolutionary movement. The *Viet Nam Phuc Quoc Hoi* [Vietnam Restoration Party], which dates from 1914 when it was established in Kwangchow, China by the late Prince Cuong De, had similar aims. Both of these clandestine organizations quickly became involved in secret conspiratorial operations that had world wide ramifications. Many of their leaders, like Prince Cuong De himself, were political exiles and took refuge in Japan. The Japanese were quite willing to serve as a base for revolutionary agitation, looking forward to a day when they might want to encourage the colonial peoples of Southeast Asia to look favorably on Japan as a leader in the area. However, lacking a legitimized outlet in Vietnam for their nationalist political activities, the *Phuc Quoc* and the *Duy Tan*, representative of a dozen or more such secret groups, developed patterns of thought and action which revolved around subversive intrigues and the use of terrorism.

The political opposition, which rested just beneath the surface during much of the French period in Vietnam, erupting violently from time to time, never partook of the qualities which distinguish it in an independent and representative republic. That is to say that the nationalist opposition of the colonial era was never likely to come to power as a responsible government. Recognition of this fact by the leaders of such groups was probably a significant factor in orienting them toward programs involving clandestine agitation, intrigue, and violence. One cannot leave this topic without noting that, even today, a great many persons in opposition to the present government of the Republic of Vietnam think and act in this same kind of framework.

The organized opposition today consists principally of members of two branches of the Dai Viet party (once influential in North Vietnam, but left with only a handful of followers in the South as a result of partition) and a relatively few members of the pre-independence *Quoc Dan Dang* [Vietnam Nationalist Party] and the *Dong Minh Hoi* [Vietnam Revolutionary League], both of which were once strong in the Center and the North. In addition, there are several other small groupings, including a weak and colorless Socialist party. Articulate oppositionists, however, are numerous and active. Some, such as Dr. Phan Huy Quat, a leader of the Dai Viet party and member of several earlier Bao Dai cabinets, have organized informal groups of likeminded intellectuals with the expressed objective of developing a core of responsible opposition to the Ngo Dinh Diem regime.[3] Others, like Dr. Phan Quang Dan, head of the recently created Republican Party and for some years a resident of Brookline, Massachusetts, played strenuous roles in the 1959 elections of the Vietnamese National Assembly.[4] Although Dr. Dan is not a member of the newly elected Assembly, there are deputies of similarly independent spirit and ideas.

The attainment of independence in 1954 opened a Pandora's box of problems and troubles for the new regime. Besides simply keeping his government alive, Ngo Dinh Diem had to make a number of difficult and important decisions. First, he had to decide whether to incorporate into the new political system the monarchy and its incumbent head, Bao Dai. If Bao Dai and the things he was thought to stand for were to be eliminated, how should this properly be done? Which of the existing administrative organs inherited from the colonial period should be retained, and which should be replaced with new ones? What would be the role of the National Army in the future development of the nation? How could the trade unions, the chambers of commerce, and the cooperatives be reoriented to the new national aims, and what should be their place in the total picture? Most important, what should the new political framework and orientation of the Free Vietnamese people be, and how could they be brought to accept and support it?

The terms Ngo Dinh Diem had stipulated as his price for taking office in June 1954 were four:

1. full civil and military powers;
2. authority to determine the future status of the country;
3. Vietnamese control of Vietnam's economy and finances;
4. freedom to establish a representative national assembly.

In return, he pledged to Bao Dai, for whom he had no admiration and who in turn had no love for him, that he would not use his grant of full powers to depose him arbitrarily; that he would instead submit the monarch's fate to the people. Although the new Prime Minister could, during the critical autumn and winter of 1954-1955, have gained enormous political capital among the fence-sitting nationalists by dramatically deposing the Chief of State (who was at that time in France) he kept his word. Despite Bao Dai's collusion with the opponents of Ngo Dinh Diem's government in the winter and spring of 1954-1955, the Prime Minister refrained from taking what many observers thought would be reasonable action against his nominal ruler until October of 1955. Then, in a nationwide referendum, Bao Dai was voted out of his position, and Ngo Dinh Diem succeeded him as chief executive of the new Republic of Vietnam.

It need hardly be pointed out that during the sixteen months between Ngo Dinh Diem's accession to power and the referendum that transformed Vietnam into a Republic, the Prime Minister and his followers did not sit idly by and wait to see what the referendum would bring. Ngo Dinh Diem had returned to Vietnam after four years of self-imposed exile, his head filled with ideas about the needs of his country and the type of political orientation it should have. Just before he left the United States for France in the summer of 1953 he told me:

> My country needs vast reforms in every field. The people must be given an opportunity for free public education in the democratic way of life. They must be taught to choose their own governmental representatives. Our administrative practices are obsolete. Our bureaucracy needs modernizing and streamlining so that it can function efficiently. Exploitation of the peasants must end and they must be shown modern

methods of agriculture. Land reform will have to be tackled in the South. The standard of living of my people is very low; it can be raised severalfold. And there must be freedom for the people to meet and argue in public places and in private without perpetual surveillance, for a free exchange of ideas is vital.

It is interesting to consider what has taken place in Vietnam in the light of this statement, although one must add that it is not altogether fair to evaluate the performance of a responsible leader in terms of his earlier thoughts as a political exile.

IV

In pre-independence Vietnam, as in most colonial countries, the nationalist political movement was marked by a number of intrinsic weaknesses, including a fundamental lack of philosophical and practical unity and an absence of agreement on programs, objectives, and world outlook. As long as the main issue was the achievement of freedom, and as long as the nationalists could leave the daily running of their country to the colonial administration, these shortcomings were not crucial. However, once independence had been secured and a transfer of power had actually taken place, they became of critical importance for the stability of the new political system.

The transfer of power in Vietnam automatically brought into being new spheres of authority and new positions of power which could not fail to have a strong influence on the economic and administrative areas of Vietnamese society. Unfortunately, in the early months of independence the Vietnamese lacked men who had had sufficient experience and sophistication to chart quickly an appropriate course of economic development for the new state. Furthermore, the immediate needs of the government were of an emergency character: settling 850,000 refugees and integrating them into the body politic of the South; shoring up the military defenses to a level of strength which would deter the Viet Cong from renewing open hostilities; and preventing rival claimants to power from overthrowing the regime by violent means. Such obviously high priority requirements made long-range economic planning of less immediate importance.

In the economic realm the absence of sufficient native capitalists and entrepreneurs rendered inescapable a large measure of state direction of the economy. (Vietnam and her sisters in Southeast Asia have, one should note, come into existence at a time when governmental direction of the economy and concentration of economic power in the hands of governments have been becoming increasingly general throughout the world.) As a corollary to this situation, the trade union movement, the cooperatives, and the Vietnamese chambers of commerce were weak and had for many years been handmaidens of the colonial regime. It is not unnatural that, to a certain extent, these organizations have remained subordinate to the political leadership of the country in the post-independence period.

In the administrative area the government of Ngo Dinh Diem has labored energetically and with some success to increase efficiency and to bring the services of the central and provincial administrations to the people. Of necessity this has resulted in a growing degree of contact between the government and the people. One might say cynically that the process of extending central government contacts with the farthermost villages carries with it a corollary extension of governmental controls and, conceivably, a correspondingly diminished area of freedom for the individual peasant and his family. This is hardly fair, however. Without communication between the government and the individual citizen it would be impossible for the Vietnamese government to assure the security and stability of the countryside and make it possible for the peasant and his family to live their lives and earn their daily bread under peaceful conditions. By the same token, it would be manifestly impossible for any Vietnamese government to develop a sturdy society unless it were able to broaden its political base and secure the active allegiance and political involvement of the masses of the population. Indeed, herein has lain one of the basic weaknesses of the Government of the Republic: it has yet to ground itself solidly in the provinces. It is at first glance somewhat ironical to argue that popular support for the Vietnamese government can be most easily assured if police and security measures in the countryside are adequate. However, given the steady pattern of terrorist attacks and assassinations in the provinces, the guerilla incursions, and the illegal collection of "taxes" by Communist cadres, given indeed the fact that the war with the Viet Cong has continued notwithstanding the armistice agreed to at Geneva in 1954, the assertion becomes understandable.

To the credit of the regime in Saigon, the well known formal steps which it has taken to erect a structure of representative government— the writing of a Constitution, the election of a National Assembly— have been supplemented by programs of community development, of agrarian reform, and of efficiently administered agricultural credit. All of these steps tend to stimulate the development of new orientations and motivations, and over a period of time should assist the growth of a sense of identity between the people and their government.

The apparent trend toward military dictatorship in South and Southeast Asia has been commented on by numerous specialists.[5] One is justified in asking whether there are at present indications of such a tendency in Vietnam. At this point the answer would be negative, notwithstanding the leadership of the November, 1960 *coup* attempt by a small group of officers. One must assume that the recent army-mounted *coups* in Korea, Pakistan, Burma, and Thailand did not pass unnoticed in Vietnam. We know, however, that Ngo Dinh Diem learned much about such possibilities during the critical months of 1954, when the then-Chief of Staff, Nguyen Van Hinh, planned to use the Army as a vehicle to power. At that time the Premier took intensive measures to reorient the thinking of the officer corps and to turn the Army into a subordinate arm of the government. In consequence, by the end of that year the National Army had become an indispensable tool for pacification of zones evacuated by the Communist (Viet Minh) forces as stipulated by the Geneva accords, as well as for rehabilitation of war-torn areas.

It is among the officers of the military services that one finds the largest cluster of Vietnamese who have thus far been exposed to American ideas and to the American scene. Many hundreds of Vietnamese officers have been taught English and then been sent to the United States for advanced military training that included standard American doctrine concerning the paramount position of the civil administration in our democratic society. This was also true, however, of officers in the Korean Army. Thus, although the Army in South Vietnam is an instrument of the civil administration today, it would be illogical to predict that Vietnamese military leaders will not at some future time engage in similar adventures. Apart from a few superficial and specious parallels, however, Vietnam is not Korea, and in the final analysis one may conclude that such a contingency is unlikely so long as the present regime's campaign against Communist forces in the South Vietnamese countryside is effective, and so long as its social and economic welfare programs bring evident benefit to the general population.

Surveying the total picture, what do we see as evidences of democratic growth in Vietnam? And what are the problems involved?

Actually, the entire issue is in a sense artificial and unrealistic. The question presupposes the desirability of democratic institutions and practices, and implicit in it is a Western conception of democracy. I am reminded of the words of Harold Nicolson:

> The Anglo-Saxon is gifted with a limitless capacity for excluding his own practical requirements from the application of the idealistic theories which he seeks to impose on others. . . . He desires to enforce upon others a standard of behavior which he would refuse to adopt himself.[6]

Of course it is not true that all Americans operate on such unspoken assumptions, but one may argue that as a nation we tend to equate what is desirable for others with what we think we have. In the life-and-death game of winning allies and influencing other peoples such a blandly unrealistic approach can be extremely dangerous.

Having said this, let us look once more at the society which is developing in the Republic of Vietnam.

On August 30, 1959, an election was held in Vietnam in which the Vietnamese people voted for their deputies to the Second National Assembly. Candidates sponsored by or favorable to the Government won a large majority of the seats. But among those present when the Assembly convened on October 5th were a number of new representatives of credibly independent character. Among the candidates were a number of outright oppositionists, whose very presence in the campaign indicated a certain degree of confidence in the honesty and sincerity of the Government. Similarly, the successful candidates included a number of bright and active young men and women, most of them educated in Western Europe or the United States, who stated their belief that the time had come for them to enter the political arena if they wanted the Vietnam of 1970 to correspond at all to their desires.

Potentially contributing to political progress in Vietnam is the dramatic westward movement of Vietnamese settlers from the overcrowded towns and villages of the plains of Annam to the wild and often unexplored reaches of the interior highlands. Twelve thousand families totaling 52,000 settlers have cleared more than 12,000 hectares of fertile forest land in the regions along the Laotian frontier. Whereas formerly many of these families struggled to eke out a tenuous living on as little as a fraction of an acre of land in Annam, today they may have as much as five hectares of productive soil per family. The opening of the West has thus not been simply a movement of several thousand families from one section of the country to another. It has meant the unfolding of new vistas, new horizons, for the Vietnamese people. The plateau regions, formerly the private hunting preserve of the Emperor, now promise almost limitless growth and expansion for the coming generation. Such a development inevitably has psychological, political, and social consequences as well as the intended economic ones.

Thousands of other families are likewise being settled on reclaimed lands in South Vietnam, with results very similar to those achieved in the highlands. In the South also, under the first major phase of the land reform program, 112,000 farm families till their own land, on acres owned before by slightly more than 1,000 persons and cultivated by tenants. The rural credit system has enabled farmers, individually or in groups, to borrow more than one billion piastres at very low interest in less than two years. The success and continuity of this program appears assured by the steady and faithful repayment of these loans.

Industrialization, too, now has its beginnings in Vietnam. Textiles, sugar refining, paper, plastics, cement, glass, and other light industries are being established or contracted for, with obvious potential social consequences.

One feels a new spirit stirring in Vietnam. The years of Republican independence have been years of relative peace, stability, and progress, although the terrorist campaigns of the Viet Cong since the summer of 1959 have seriously obstructed some of the administration's programs. The Vietnamese see new schools being built in villages across the land, dams being constructed to irrigate tens of thousands of acres where water has always been scarce and productivity limited, dikes being erected for the rehabilitation of vast areas formerly rendered infertile periodically by the ravages of the sea. In almost every province new roads are being cut to bring isolated villages closer to their neighbors and to the safety that comes with ease of communication. The Trans-Vietnam railway has been restored, bridging a 500-kilometer gap resulting from war-damage. The process of national reconstruction is quickening its pace.

Yet one would be naive to suppose that these developments, however significant, will bring democracy to a country whose population lacks both a democratic tradition and a widespread understanding of the Hellenic and Anglo-Saxon experience. As President Ngo Dinh Diem has put it:

> Democracy is not a group of texts and laws to be read and applied. It is essentially a state of mind, a way of living with the utmost respect toward every human being, ourselves as well as our neighbors. It requires constant self-education, careful practice, flexible and patient attention, in order to achieve a harmonious balance between the desirably diverse conceptions of men and the inevitable complexity of reality. Democracy demands from each of us, then, infinitely greater efforts, understanding and goodwill than any other form of government. . . .[7]

If we are to judge developments in Vietnam we must do so in its own context—not by comparison with our own twentieth-century standards, but against the situation that obtained in Vietnam before President Ngo assumed office, and what has occurred in neighboring Asian countries in recent years. Using either yardstick, the achievements of the Ngo Dinh Diem Government in respect to democratic development constitute a positive and commendable record. Nevertheless, serious problems do exist, the resolution of which may well determine the character of Vietnamese society in the years ahead.

The principal task of democratic development in Vietnam is to create broad social support for the varied and sometimes conflicting institutions and programs assumed to be necessary for the continued functioning and improvement of the society. The Constitution of the Republic itself contains elements which, if sustained by practice over the years, can assist democratic growth. It contains a statement of the fundamental civil rights of the Vietnamese citizen and the obligation of the government to assist him in the enjoyment of those rights, as well as an assurance to him of equality of opportunity with his fellows. The Constitution also sets forth the citizen's obligations, including his responsibility to support the nation's principles: "the republican form of government, the democratic regime, national freedom, independence, and unity." True, the document's bill of rights is qualified by the cautious clauses found in the constitutions of many recently organized states, offering the government legal means to salvage state power if at any time it seems to be threatened by the unrestricted exercise of these rights. All in all, however, there is nothing in its content to inhibit the development of a sturdy representative regime, so long as that is the intent of the country's leaders. The point may be made that the national leadership, under the Constitution, is vested in a strong executive. However, this is the first tendency one usually observes in newly independent states in Asia and Africa. One may object to such a development on theoretical grounds as essentially undemocratic, but in practice it is a logical consequence of the need of the new governments to assure their continued existence and keep their administrative machines operating smoothly. In Vietnam, it is likely to continue as long as the Communist threat to the Republic remains "clear and present."

Corollary to the strength of the executive branch in the new states is the presence of weak, passive, or subservient judicial and legislative branches; here again Vietnam runs fairly close to type. This does not mean that the National Assembly is completely ineffectual, but that it is still too new and inexperienced an element in the structure of the government to have evolved into a balance or mediator between the executive and the people. This situation is also related to the absence in Vietnam of an organized, responsible, political opposition that can be effectively represented in the legislature. Nor does Vietnam have a tradition of an independent judiciary, and one cannot say that it is overstaffed with brilliant jurists.

It is difficult for a foreign observer to assess the depth or intensity of the desire of the Vietnamese for a democratic society. President Ngo Dinh Diem and members of his official family have recorded their intention to lead the nation toward such a society. Against such pledges, however, the observer finds he must weigh and balance the frequently heard criticisms of "police-state" activities undertaken or sanctioned by the regime. Freedom of the press, for instance, is an issue hotly and often discussed among intellectuals in Vietnam today. The issue is not solely of current origin, since during the years of French colonial rule the press was pre-censored by the Government General. Following the granting of "independence" to the regime of Bao Dai in 1949, Premier Tran Van Huu put renewed emphasis on pre-censorship of the press[8] and increased pressure on it in an effort to secure its support for the new Government. Under subsequent administrations press censorship continued, as did other related controls such as licensing of publications, regulation of publishing and circulation procedures, and allocation of newsprint.

When Ngo Dinh Diem took office as Prime Minister in July, 1954, the penalties for violation of the censorship regulations became less stringent. Punishments ranged from reprimands to revocations of licenses to publish, but no publishers were fined or imprisoned; the evident trend was toward greater press freedom. Foreign correspondence, which had been strictly controlled by French military censors during the years of civil strife, was freed from censorship in August, 1954. In February, 1956, pre-censorship of Vietnamese language papers was officially abolished, but was continued for non-Vietnamese (i.e., Chinese and French) publications.

The honeymoon between the press and Vietnam's first sovereign regime in nearly a century gradually came to an end, however, as Vietnamese journalists increasingly criticized government acts in news stories and editorials, and an abnormally sensitive governmental leadership reacted to "journalistic irresponsibility" by imposing once more a measure of official supervision and control over publication content. By the spring of 1958 the publisher of a leading Saigon daily had been fined by the courts and the offending issue of his paper seized for (a) having published news "likely to encourage Communism" in Vietnam, and (b) having slandered the economic police service.[9] The year 1959 saw further evidences of a lack of rapport between the Government and the press. One Saigon newspaper was suspended because of its editor's alleged moral and financial misconduct,[10] another because it had been found guilty by a Saigon tribunal of libel.[11] Furthermore, although pre-censorship was not restored, the control of the Vietnamese Veterans Association, a semi-autonomous government agency, over the distribution of all publications in the Republic had a tempering effect on editorial inclinations. And, too, "popular" demonstrations against newspapers which have been especially critical of the regime have tended to inhibit the development of a spirit of free criticism.

One hears rumors in Saigon of reported acts of corruption by government officials. Any student of history recognizes the near-universality of such accusations. In the case of Vietnam, corruption was a clearly marked feature of the colonial period, and Ngo Dinh Diem's advent to power in 1954 brought a general reaction from the country's bureaucracy. For all the doubts entertained as to his capacity to solve the myriad critical problems he faced, no doubt was voiced as to his integrity, nor as to his reputation for refusing to countenance corruption among his associates and subordinates. Indeed, whatever the word-picture that Vietnamese and foreign journalists and observers drew of Ngo Dinh Diem in 1954, the appellation "a man of undisputed integrity" was always included in the characterization. However, on taking power, the new chief of government found that his reputation for incorruptibility had either frightened or alienated many key civil servants in the administration he had inherited. The hostility of many of the ranking French-oriented bureaucrats was so evident that a civil service "Court of Honor" ordinance promulgated by the Prime Minister late in the summer of 1954, which would have required all government employees to declare all their assets under oath, was quietly shelved. It was considered more vital at that time for the new regime to win the support and active cooperation of the bureaucracy, and to keep the administrative machine functioning, than to begin a general housecleaning.

Since the start of 1958, however, President Ngo has taken an increasingly stern position on corruption. The country's newspapers have carried one account after another of officials, army officers, and contractors brought before the courts for taking bribes, misappropriating public funds, and similar crimes. Even former cabinet ministers and officers ranking as high as major general have been so charged and convicted (often in absentia, for many fled the country to escape prosecution).[12] Nevertheless, charges of corruption against persons high in the administration of the regime, as well as against members of the President's family, persist, and because the Government has not found a means of effectively refuting them, its reputation at home and abroad has been damaged.

Charges of *gouvernement en famille*—or nepotism—have also been levelled at the regime of Ngo Dinh Diem. These accusations, admittedly ugly, refer to the fact that the President's principal political adviser is his younger brother, Ngo Dinh Nhu, and that the major political figure in Central Vietnam is another younger brother, Ngo Dinh Can. Neither occupies an official governmental post. Such accusations are suggestive of a certain cozily unclean character to the Saigon administration and they find willing listeners.[13] Yet, appointments of relatives to governmental office or reliance upon one's immediate family for political advice and assistance are not without precedent in Vietnamese history—nor, for that matter, in the history of any nation. Furthermore, in an emerging political society such as that of Vietnam, the limited extent of literacy and higher education, the narrow range of political sophistication, and the habit (from colonial times) of thinking of political action in terms of intrigue, of subversion, and of reliance upon those on whose loyalty one could depend, all work to encourage government by a tight elite. Indeed, it is difficult to conceive of *any* regime in Vietnam which would not include several members of the family or families comprising its leadership.

It is interesting that some of the Government's most outspoken critics took an active and open part in the recent electoral compaigns. It is significant also that few persons in the capital city of Saigon, for instance, appear to have inhibitions about criticizing the Government openly in the bars or even on the sidewalks. Furthermore, the clearly relaxed relationship that has developed in the past five years between the citizenry of Saigon-Cholon and the municipal police (this has been remarked by casual travelers as well as expert observers) suggests that accusations of authoritarianism lack solid substance. Again, one notes an increase of *responsible* criticism in the newspapers, and professional publications more and more contain reflections on problems of governmental efficiency, as well as frequent exhortations to ranking officials to "take the government to the people."

Indeed, one notes that the bulk of the criticisms coming from responsible oppositionists and from thoughtful young scholars and administrators concern the failure of the regime to build its base of support in two of the most vital areas of the nation: in the villages and among the intellectuals. There is reason to believe that the Government enjoys whole-hearted support from a large majority of the population. There is also reason to believe that it has something less than that in some districts of certain provinces. There may be many reasons for this, as, for instance, the weakness of communication and of communications: (1) there is a failure on the part of the central government to maintain constant and satisfying contact with the communes and the villages; and (2) the country still lacks sufficient and adequate avenues of physical transportation connecting the capital and the countryside.

The first of these gaps is slowly being closed. At the President's insistence, province and district chiefs are expected to spend a good part of their work week journeying about their zones of responsibility, learning the problems of the people. Even so, one must recognize that many government services have not yet reached the mass of the people in rural areas. This, combined with a still low (though improving) literacy rate, absence of sufficient newspapers outside the capital city,[14] and a lack of enough radios, prevents large numbers of people from being kept aware that they now have a central government which is *theirs*, and not that of a foreign power. Thus it is difficult to convince many of these people that the President and his ministers and officials know about them and their problems and care about them. The President himself has made frequent tours of the Republic since he took office in 1954, and has visited some provinces five and even six times or more. But the task of bringing the "heart" of government to the people whom it is designed to serve cannot be accomplished by one man alone.

As for the intelligentsia, the basic problem here stems from their feeling left out of the ruling group. Certainly it is verifiable that many teachers, students, writers, and other intellectuals and quasi-intellectuals have been alienated by some of the Government's policies. Of course, in a revolutionary epoch a certain amount of alienation is probably inevitable. Again, one must note that many intellectuals in Vietnam are fearful of possible persecution; some are simply passive in their reactions to the Government; many others are openly hostile. Their attitudes may sometimes be conditioned by frustrated ambitions (as was true of a former functionary of sub-cabinet rank, who boasted publicly in 1955 that he could command the loyalty of most of the civil service, and that if he were not given either the Ministry of Defense or of the Interior he would simply call the civil servants out on strike and take over the entire government as Prime Minister). But it is also apparently true that the administration has not taken particular pains to win them over to its cause. Although the leaders of the government are themselves educated professional men, their propaganda appeals have been directed to the mass of the people. Little attention has been paid to discontented literati, nor has the government's official "personalist" ideology been broached in terms likely to attract their adherence.

In the last analysis it is clear that the growth of democratic institutions in a country such as Vietnam will be dependent upon the goodwill and intentions of its leadership. While President Ngo Dinh Diem has gone on record as favoring a "democratic structure" in Vietnam, built out of a "genuine respect for the dignity of the individual,"[15] we must not forget that there is no democratic tradition in Vietnam, and that its level of political sophistication is not high. Furthermore, the young Republic is now entering on a period of economic development which will probably result in many integral changes in its society, and there will be many necessary adjustments to changing conditions and changing needs. Furthermore, this long-term process will be directed initially by the government itself. While one may accept at face value President Ngo Dinh Diem's high motivation and sincerity of intention, one must also recognize that certain economic decisions of political and social import will necessarily be taken without consulting the people, possibly without even considering their wishes.

Western democracy assumes the presence of an informed and enlightened electorate. The literacy programs and expanded educational efforts undertaken by the Vietnamese Government may eventually produce such an electorate. The measures now being taken by the Government to bring every district in the country into contact with its neighbors and with the capital, and to bring the services of the administration to the most remote villages will also help. If Vietnam is permitted to benefit from a few more years of peaceful development and growth, a new generation will enter the political picture: educated, informed, and, we may hope, philosophically oriented toward the institutions of freedom. These could be the builders of a democratic society in Free Vietnam. It is they who may finally transform the dreams and hopes of their fathers into reality.

---

[1] Although France formally handed over her civil powers in Vietnam to the Saigon government on September 17, 1954, she continued to pay subsidies to the armies of the Sects until March, 1955. (*New York Times*, March 12, 1955.)

[2] During the abortive *coup* of November 10-11, 1960, only a few hundred soldiers (paratroopers stationed in the capital city area) went into rebellion; the uprising was put down by other units of the 150,000-man army.

[3] On April 30, 1960, eighteen political personalities and intellectuals released to the press the text of a petition they had sent to President Ngo on April 26. The petition, which called for various "reforms," was purportedly prepared some time earlier than the date of its release, but there are indications that its publication was stimulated by a desire to ride the tide of inter-

national interest that attended the overthrow of the Rhee administration in Korea a short time earlier. The petition was signed by Dr. Quat and also by several other well known nationalists. The majority of the signers, however, were earlier identified with the Hoa Hao, Cao Dai, and Binh Xuyen groups, or had been cabinet ministers under the French-sponsored regime of Bao Dai. With only a few exceptions, these members of the non-Communist opposition were not involved in the attempted *coup* of November 1960.

⁴ Dr. Dan was victorious in his district (Saigon No. 2), but his success was invalidated by the courts on the grounds that he had (1) bribed voters and (2) violated the election laws. Dr. Dan's disqualification in this fashion was received with dismay by foreign observers. It also endowed him with a martyr-like quality which certainly had not been intended by the Saigon administration. At the height of the November 1960 *coup* attempt, Dr. Dan came to the fore as self-designated "adviser" and "spokesman" for the rebel leadership, and when this effort to overthrow the Ngo Dinh Diem regime failed, he was jailed.

⁵ See, for example, Guy J. Pauker, "Southeast Asia as a Problem Area in the Next Decade," *World Politics*, April, 1959, pp. 325-345.

⁶ *Peacemaking, 1919* (Boston and New York, 1933), p. 193.

⁷ Proclamation of the Republic, October 26, 1955.

⁸ Decree 81-SG/PTT, May 19, 1950.

⁹ Action was taken under a law of the Bao Dai regime, never repealed, providing for the seizure of any newspaper making propaganda for Communism.

¹⁰ *Nguoi Viet Tu Do*, whose editor was the defendant in two trials for swindling and was also sentenced for issuing a check without sufficient funds. (*Le Journal d'Extrème Orient*, June 5, 1959).

¹¹ *Dan Nguyen* was convicted of having libeled the Department of Education; its editorial management were fined and the paper suspended from publication for one month. (*Vietnam Press*, English language edition, August 21, 1959).

¹² See, for example, *Yuan Tung Jih Pao* (Cholon, Chinese), March 20, 1958; *Tieng Chuong* (Saigon, Vietnamese), September 12, 1958; *Tu Do* (Saigon, Vietnamese), October 11, 1958; *Ngon Luan* (Saigon, Vietnamese), November 22, 1958; *Dan Nguyen* (Saigon, Vietnamese), November 29, 1958; *Tin Moi* (Saigon, Vietnamese), December 13, 1958; *Tu Do*, January 8, 1959.

¹³ Mme Ngo Dinh Nhu, wife of the Political Advisor to the President, is probably the most frequently criticized member of the family. Bright, vivacious, and a passionate feminist, Mme Nhu is a member of the National Assembly and the author of a much-discussed "family law" (Law No. 1/59, January 2, 1959), which prohibited concubinage and virtually banned divorce in the Republic. MM. Nhu and Can, together with Mme Nhu, have often been accused of corruption as a consequence of their reputed involvement in commercial transactions. Investigations of such charges, however, have not brought forth evidence that any of the family has been personally enriched. Rather, it has been asserted that they have engaged in these activities for the purpose of providing financing for the *Can Lao Nhan Vy*, which has no other means of support. However, the clandestine character of their enterprises stimulates speculation. The factor in the situations of MM. Nhu and Can which lends itself most easily to criticism is the absence of any official or stated limitation to their authority. The vagueness of their status gives rise to rumors and lends credence to accusations of their abuse of power. It is difficult to come to grips with criticisms of this sort in rational political terms. There is no denying, however, that even if no abuse of power and no corruption exist, the very fact of such family relationships at the locus of power cannot but engender an atmosphere of distrust and thereby render the regime more susceptible to attack.

¹⁴ Although nine Vietnamese languages dailies (circulation est. 217,000) and ten Chinese language papers (circulation est. 45,000) are published in Saigon-Cholon, there are as yet no provincial newspapers in Vietnam.

¹⁵ E. g., his address at the Inauguration of the First Session of the National Assembly, March 15, 1956.

CHAPTER 3

Personalism in Vietnam

*by John C. Donnell**

INTRODUCTION

In a Saigon public square in early 1956 a white-suited official lit an unusual bonfire. The flames licked at a huge pile of confiscated porno-graphic publications, playing cards, and opium pipes and lamps. Public attention was thus drawn to the "Anti-Four Vices Campaign" to eradi-cate "the social vestiges of the feudal and colonial regimes." The cam-paign was one phase of the Ngo government's "personalist" (*nhan-vi*) movement to revive the best elements of traditional Vietnamese culture and to present them in combination with certain values of Western civ-ilization as a systematic philosophical basis for national reconstruction. An alternate translation of *nhan-vi*[1] is "humanist," and the doctrine in fact attempts to link basic theistic and humanist values of East and West. Vietnamese personalism is heavily influenced by the French Catholic *personnalisme* of Jacques Maritain and especially of Emmanuel Mounier and his *revue Esprit* group, but Vietnamese officials contend that their personalism is not connected necessarily with any religion. Personalism with its humanist and spiritual emphases is conceived to be philosoph-ical antidote to materialistic, atheistic Communism, but the Vietnamese are understandably reluctant to refer to it as an "ideology." President Ngo has, however, referred to it as a new national "formula."

Years before the 1954-1955 crisis many non-Communist Vietnamese nationalists were gravely concerned by the successes of Viet Minh prop-aganda in its highly systematized Marxist framework, and thus came to feel a need to formulate their own "ideological" position. When they

*John C. Donnell is currently a member of the Center for Southeast Asia Studies, Institute of International Studies, University of California. He served in Vietnam with the United States Information Service, 1950-1952 and 1955-1957. Portions of this paper originally appeared in the author's "National Renovation Campaigns in Vietnam" in *Pacific Affairs* (XXXII, No. 1 [March, 1959]), whose permission to include them here is gratefully acknowledged.

perceived after the Geneva pact of 1954 that independence from the French was not the panacea that many had imagined, they became more concerned than ever with the problem of developing something immediately applicable in a "dynamic" new nationalist credo of their own.

Soon after assuming the reins of government in July, 1954, Ngo Dinh Diem and his brothers (who constitute a sort of informal privy council for him) decided that among the most pressing immediate problems facing the new regime were moral lassitude and the weakening of government authority among the people. Vietnam had passed through a cataclysmic period of rapid change and turmoil. Her traditional values had been condemned, and substitutes had been offered in such developments as the French colonization of the country, the Japanese occupation, and the establishment in North Vietnam of Ho Chi Minh's Communist state dedicated to the obliteration of Confucian influence and much of traditional morality. There had been also the long military struggle against the Viet Minh and the rise of the politico-military sects in the South which variously espoused a new eclectic religious cult (Cao Dai), a new native variant of Buddhism (Hoa Hao) and militarized gangsterism with fraternal trappings (Binh Xuyen). Soon after accepting the premiership, Ngo spoke of his resolve to attack this general problem: ". . . beside the legacy of past foreign domination and war who among us can claim he has no responsibility in the moral crisis of today? Each of us must search his own soul. . ."[2]

The Ngo family is Roman Catholic and its adherence to Christianity has increased its interest in the possibilities of combining Vietnamese with Western cultural values. Significantly, their father was educated in both Vietnam and Malaya and founded a school in Hue which was the first in the country to initiate "a modern system of education based on the combination of western and eastern cultures." Young Ngo Dinh Diem went to this school after he had gone through "a system of both French and Vietnamese education, at the Pellerin School in Hue."[3]

President Ngo and two of his four brothers have been in the forefront of the various campaigns to restore vigor to the traditional Vietnamese virtues in public life and to propagate personalism. Ngo Dinh Nhu is Political Advisor to the President and is considered to be the leading theorist of the Vietnamese personalist movement. He was evidently first attracted to the doctrine while studying in France in the 1930's. His wife is a leader of women's groups and a deputy in the National Assembly where she introduced the controversial Family Bill discussed below. Monseigneur Ngo Dinh Thuc, Archbishop of Hue, was formerly Bishop of Vinh Long where the Personalism Training Center was started early in 1957.

MORALITY CAMPAIGNS AND THE REVIVAL OF CONFUCIANISM

A semi-official source has pointed out that the emphasis on moral government in Vietnam has traditionally been part of a political ideal of rule by an enlightened monarch and bureaucracy and not "by the people or their representatives." This system worked because public office was "open to all, by way of competitive examination" and also "because there was a strict moral code and . . . on the whole the government had a strong sense of public duty and responsibility to the people." President Ngo's problem, then, was to give Vietnam "a solid moral basis on which to rebuild a strong, healthy, democratic state."[4] In promulgating the Constitution on October 26, 1956, Ngo said: "It behooves us now to restore the spirit of public service, the spirit of honor and of national dignity, moral and intellectual honesty, the spirit of sacrifice, the sense of discipline, and personal responsibility, courtesy in human relations which is simply the expression of respect for others as for oneself."[5] He recommended two traditional virtues: *thanh* ("intellectual loyalty and noble morality, an acute consciousness of and clear vision of . . . one's duties . . .") and *tin* (the "sincere and courageous" practice of those duties and one's responsibilities). These Confucian concepts (not identified as such by Ngo) had been extolled by Vietnamese scholars through the ages and had been treated in detail by a noted writer, Pham Quynh, for example, some 20 years before.[6]

There has been a Confucian type of emphasis on the moral example of the ruler. In political slogans and tracts Ngo was frequently called *chi-si*, meaning "a man of will, of determination, of decision, of character." The President protested against this practice in late 1954, and after additional remonstrances it declined after late 1955. He was frequently held up by the government's Information Department as worthy of emulation by the Vietnamese people, as in the following newspaper comment of early 1957: "To better the civil servant's status and fight against bribery, the President gives a good example with his simple and sober life. . ."[7] At this time, government personnel were holding meetings to study the President's "life and his work" and "his revolutionary virtues."[8] The patriotic song *Suy-Ton Ngo Tong-Thong* ["Venerate President Ngo"], which came to be called the "second national anthem," was routinely played in the theaters, causing grumbling among the public which had the impression that this was done on government orders. Actually the President, who rarely goes to a theater, was unaware that the practice had continued after he had very early expressed his dissatisfaction with it, and two more subsequent objections on his part were required to end it.

The government-supported *Times of Vietnam* in December, 1956 expressed gratification at seeing "the gradual but firm suppression of a budding cult of personality which has resulted from an excess of zeal on the part of some admirers of the President." It said Ngo had declined to allow his name to be used to rename the Khai Dinh secondary school in Hue, preferring to revive its older name of *Quoc Hoc* [National School]. Some government publication, such as *Vietnam Press*, continued even later to incline to fulsome reporting, as in a news story that a group had listened to a speech by the President "in a quasi-religious silence."9

One of the formal morality campaigns attempted to revitalize the bureaucracy taken over from the colonial regime. A "Week of Diligence in the Administrative Services" was observed in August, 1955, as a start toward stirring civil servants out of their former status of "automaton, slave of routine." Functionaries were urged "to be close to the people," not to resort to flattery but to be "just and magnanimous, to make themselves respected and loved" and finally to be "just and humane" in applying regulations. A pamphlet of this period for government employees on improvement of work methods suggested ways to modernize office routines and also discussed four main administrative weaknesses: carelessness, bureaucratism, egocentrism, and laziness. It also urged the cultivation of four virtues: *nhan* and *nghia* [humanity and righteousness or justice, called earlier by Pham Quynh the "fundamental virtues of the Confucian ethic"], *liem* [honesty or integrity], and *tin* [sincerity and reliability, defined by Ngo Dinh Diem above].

Meanwhile a campaign against corruption had been launched. In about the fall of 1954, a "code of honor" had been established as a standard of ethics for civil servants. The government set up a commission to examine the personal financial situations of all applicants for army and administrative posts to facilitate any future investigations which might be necessary. The press reported prominently in August, 1955 the prosecution for extortion of a provincial official and a Buddhist priest accomplice, and noted that all judicial personnel had been informed of the facts and each had been invited to "meditate on the case and to make his own examination of conscience." Two spectacular cases of graft were turned up in 1956 in the Ministry of National Economy and the National Bank along with smaller cases elsewhere. President Ngo had promised earlier that deserving and model functionaries would be rewarded, and some government decorations were reported to have been awarded to such men in the following months.

A vigorous "anti-embezzlement law" was promulgated in April, 1959 providing a possible death sentence for embezzlement of sums over two million piastres, as well as life imprisonment and lighter penalties for lesser offenses. An offender's property may be totally or partially confiscated and a receiver of stolen property or funds given the same sentence as the embezzler.[10] Acknowledging the severity of the law, the *Times of Vietnam* commented that it should be modified eventually "when corruption is no longer the rule but only the exception."[11] Another campaign was conducted in the armed forces through lectures and other indoctrination materials. President Ngo aided in this, and in at least one speech described the "traditional virtues of the military."

The "Anti-Four Vices Campaign" launched in late 1955 was aimed at opium-smoking, alcoholism, prostitution, and gambling. Poster exhibits and dramatic skits on the evils of vice were sent around the country. For awhile in late 1956 it appeared that restaurants and bars might be limited to serving liquor only during mealtimes,[12] and youths were reported to have been arrested for wearing "cowboy" clothing with "pipe-stem" trousers and "loud" sports shirts. In January, 1958, President Ngo commented that a social welfare conference in Tokyo had been surprised to hear of "the successful eradication of the four social plagues" in Vietnam.[13] However, news reports from Saigon have continued to describe government measures to combat prostitution.[14]

As part of the campaign for reviving Confucianism the anniversary of Confucius was proclaimed an official Vietnamese holiday in 1956 for the first time in the modern period.[15] A Vietnam Confucian Association was organized in Saigon in February, 1957, its manifesto claiming that Confucianism was timely even in the atomic age because it taught that "people must change according to the nature of their era to conform to the laws of evolution of human society." It called for public support to establish "a purely Vietnamese culture, using Confucianism as the foundation and science for public service. . ."[16] Interest in reviving Confucianism seemed to be increasing in Vietnam, at least among government officials. The anniversary observances of 1957 and 1958 were on a progressively larger scale and emphasized speeches, dances by schoolgirls, and sports events. The annual literary competition of Confucian inspiration was revived in 1957. In 1958, the only living direct descendant of Confucius traveled from Taiwan at the request of the Vietnamese association to give a series of lectures throughout Vietnam. President Ngo customarily makes the principal speech at the annual Confucian ceremonies. The rebuilding of Confucian and other temples and historical monuments has become an important concern of the Vietnamese government which alloted ten million piastres for this purpose in March, 1958.[17] Ngo Dinh Nhu personally worked to expedite this "conservation of the national cultural patrimony."[18]

VIETNAMESE PERSONALISM AND THE EUROPEAN PERSONALIST INFLUENCE

These activities to eradicate vice and restore traditional values constituted the groundwork for the personalist movement. Since 1956 the Ngo brothers and officials high and low in the government have referred to personalism (and humanism) as the philosophical basis of the national revolution. The following clause is part of the Preamble to the Constitution: "Confident in the transcendent values of the human person whose free, harmonious and complete development on the individual as well as on the communal plane must be the object of all state activity. . ." Among the national aspirations are "the erection, in the respect for the human person, for the benefit of all classes of the population, of a political, economic, social and cultural democratic regime."

In its basic conception of man's role in society and the universe, Vietnamese personalism appears to accord with French Catholic *personnalisme* as expounded by the neo-Thomist philosopher Jacques Maritian and particularly the late Emmanuel Mounier and his colleagues on *Esprit*, the monthly journal which Mounier founded in 1932. Maritain's and Mounier's personalist philosophies are not easy to summarize briefly.[19] They are a reaction against the "depersonalized," anonymous quality of modern life as influenced by machine technology, mass society, and the rise of such collectivist movements as communism and fascism. The Christian Democratic movements in half a dozen European countries are based in varying degrees on elements of personalist philosophy.[20]

Mounier's personalism combined neo-Thomism with a Marxian economic analysis of the weaknesses of capitalism which a "necessary revolution" should replace by a new kind of socialism. The columns of *Esprit* are open to Protestants and agnostics as well as Catholics. The movement twice suffered some preliminary threat of Church condemnation (1933 and 1936) but the danger passed—"On the left of the left within the Church there stood and stands *Esprit*."[21]

Mounier considered the person a unique, creative entity which cannot be regarded as merely a unit in a collective whole. The person develops by "confrontation" with the difficult problems of life and by creative, independent decision-making. In his emphasis on man's independence and responsibility for his own actions, Mounier provided an instance of the "close similarity between the preoccupations of Existentialists and Personalists." He identified a true existentialist tradition in such men as Jaspers, Berdyaev, Buber, and the Christian existentialist Gabriel Marcel, but he condemned the atheistic existentialism of Sartre which holds that man is so autonomous as to be able to "re-create" himself by his step of adhesion to a higher set of values. In Mounier, man "affirms" himself through such a process of reflective self-disclosure, but instead of merely becoming what he makes of himself as in the Sartrean formula, he is defined by the Catholic doctrinal concept of human nature. However, Mounier insisted that this "fundamental humanism" in Catholic doctrine must be purged of "all the evils which bourgeois civilization has brought into it."

French and Vietnamese personalist tracts disclose a Thomist emphasis on man's possession of reason which frees him from a helpless dependence on his animal instincts and sets him above the lower forms of life. The terms *nhan-vi* and *personne humaine* convey the dignity of the human position as the highest on the scale of natural beings below the Almighty. Man has a material aspect as well as the spiritual one based on the existence of his immortal soul but personalists emphasize the "primacy of the spiritual." Thus, "spiritualism" is the way for man to avoid the errors of "materialism," "individualism" and "idealism." Individualism here refers to a selfish conception impelling each individual to develop his own personality at the expense of others. The contrast between *person* and *individual* here is shown in the tenet that the person develops as he purifies himself of the individual within him. Idealism here refers to various philosophical conceptions regarding man as a mere instrument of impersonal forces in history, or denying corporeal substance and therefore tending to slight the importance of man's material needs.

Marxist materialism is rejected as a one-sided view of man's nature, slighting his spiritual needs. However, the French and Vietnamese personalist position on capitalism follows important parts of the Marxist critique of the quantitative, impersonal goal of profit and the alienation of the worker by depriving him not only of his own product but of his own labor which he should devote in greater portion to the development of his potentialities as a person. Personalists hold that such development will come through a different kind of profits-distribution system that gives workers a larger share, and also from widened opportunities ·for workers to participate in industrial management and thus develop greater initiative and responsibility. Mounier agreed with Marx's theory of the inevitable trend of capitalist systems toward imperialism and internal cyclical collapse. Mounier and Maritain have both written that capitalism would have to be superseded before a personalist society could be realized. On this "necessary revolution," Mounier said "direct pressures" by the people might be important means, including strikes, boycotts, insurrections, etc.,[22] but these are not mentioned in Vietnamese personalist tracts.

Collectivization is regarded by European personalists as a force for good insofar as large, powerful institutions can guarantee human rights, but also as a force to be controlled to prevent its invading the personal domain. If certain public services must be nationalized, Mounier wrote, the personalist ideal of a decentralized economy is compromised. Although he called his ideal a new version of socialism, neither he nor other French personalists have been doctrinaire socialists because they consider many socialist movements too materialistic in their preoccupation with economic solutions, and also because the personalists fear too great a concentration of power in an ordinary socialist government and its party bureaucracy.

To prevent state encroachment in the personal domain, French personalists prescribe social pluralism along with economic decentralization. Natural social groups and formations such as the family, labor unions, political parties, churches, businesses, schools, colleges, towns, provinces, etc. are to be protected and regulated by the state. But the state is enjoined not to try to substitute its comparatively artificial type of initiative for theirs, which is considered more natural and spontaneous. (Religious and non-religious groups would be permitted to operate their own schools.) The balance between social and individual priorities is set according to the neo-Thomist view (Maritain's is widely cited) of the function of law in reconciling man's individual rights with the common good. Personalists regard their position on these social questions as antithetical to the Communist version of human fulfillment found in the total submergence of the individual in the collective will and goals of the party.

There are strong similarities between these ideals and the policy statements of the personalist-oriented *Mouvement républican populaire* (MRP), the post-liberation organization of French Christian Democracy. A young *Esprit* militant, Gilbert Dru, provided the original impetus during the German occupation of France for discussions and contacts which led to the decision to form the MRP.[23]

Pluralist demands are much less prominent in the Vietnamese personalist movement than in the French. Vietnam, along with other new nations, is confronted with the very different problem of increasing the people's sense of nationhood and national political loyalty. Newly created social organizations in Vietnam usually possess a secondary, political function of expressing or confirming loyalty to the government, as contrasted with the politically more neutral "intermediary" function of such groups in older Western pluralist societies. Even so, Ngo Dinh Nhu reveals a theoretical orientation towards a pluralist ideal when he says that Vietnamese personalism advocates the "moral armament" of the citizen to enable him to withstand all political, economic, and social pressures and then specifically cites the strongest of these pres- sures as those of the government.[24]

President Ngo has spoken of intermediary groups in Vietnamese personalism as follows:

> Our society rests on two pillars: the family and the community. It is up to us to complete this traditional socio-political duality by the coordinated addition of a third element, cooperative organizations, economic units functioning to ensure the necessary material conditions for the integrated life of the family and administrative units of the community.[25]

Social and economic programs of the personalist French Christian Democratic movement show resemblances and even some organizational affiliation with those in Vietnam. Some personalist guidelines are being furnished through demographic surveys conducted in Vietnam by National Bank officials and the French Dominican research group, *Economie et Humanisme*. The latter, founded in 1942, "represents a kind of left-wing offshoot of Christian Democracy," and its goals for France have included voluntary peasant groupings for cooperative production.[26] Father Louis Lebret, former U.N. economist and head of the group's research center, has estimated the Vietnamese population's growth rate at 1.8 per cent per year and has predicted an increase of 56 per cent over the next 25 years. On the basis of this growth and a desired increase in per capita consumption, Lebret has suggested a long-range objective of doubling production in 25 years by an average production increase of three per cent per year.[27] (Such Christian Democratic lay groups in France as the *Jeunesse agricole chrétienne* or JAC have made regional surveys for the preparation of important monographs on rural problems such as the need for adequate specialized education, improved housing and recreational facilities, and the placement of young families on farms of their own.)[28]

Naturally there are differences in the emphasis of personalist doctrine and its application in Vietnam and France. Mounier himself called personalism a perspective and a challenging view of life, rather than a set of specific answers to social questions. Concrete policy recommendations drawn from such philosophical interpretations can and have varied considerably. Mounier's own viewpoints were not always accepted universally even in European personalist circles where he enjoyed a wide influence. In 1948, for example, the London Personalist Group[29] disagreed with a Mounier commentary condemning Stalinism but maintaining that the Soviet Union had achieved "the necessary revolution" and would move toward freedom while capitalist America, still facing her gravest internal crisis, would inevitably lead the West toward imperialism and war.

Despite such differences, there is a basic doctrinal consistency between these various personalist movements and particularly between the Vietnamese and French. The basic personalist values, centering on the potential freedom and creativity of the person and including the integration of the family, the outward impulsion of the person toward other persons and toward God, the necessary limitation on individual freedom in consideration of the social good, the middle way between totalitarianism and excessively individualistic liberalism, the importance assigned to development of the person's initiative and responsibility through his work activity with a consequent downgrading of the profit goal of economic enterprise—all these are among values integral to the Vietnamese movement as well as the French.

OFFICIAL STATEMENTS EMBODYING PERSONALIST DOCTRINE

President Ngo's 1956 speech dealing with the constitutional problem is a good example of the Vietnamese personalist perspective on national affairs. In it, the President defined the central problem in man's relations to society as the reconciling of the individual's liberty with the collective demands of his society. He pointed to the weaknesses of eighteenth- and nineteenth-century Western liberal democratic theories "in which individualism and economic liberalism were advocated as proper formulas to emancipate man and to lead mankind toward happiness. While this system brought relative freedom to a minority of its citizens, at the same time it lessened the effectiveness of the state, which became impotent to defend collective interests and to solve social problems." These weaknesses were revealed glaringly in the period between the two world wars, the President continued, when they led to the establishment of fascist and communist states based on the "pretext of organizing power effectively [to achieve] social justice."

Meanwhile, in the democratic regimes, "an important current of ideas has . . . led thinkers and jurists to revise the basic notions of modern democracies, as well as their methods and structures." He said:

> Most democratic states have endeavored, either by constitutional changes or by legislative enactment, to modify their political institutions. . . . Although they have been diverse, these transformations of Public Law which aim at reconciling the demands of collective discipline and social justice with those of individual liberty reveal a personalistic tendency. In addition to the negative liberties of a political nature, it is recognized that the human person has positive freedoms, . . . of an economic and social nature. At the same time the state, organized on a more democratic basis, is given a wider, more stable and more effective grant of power to bring positive assistance to the citizen against the massive dangers of materialist civilization, and to guarantee to him the right to live and exercise his liberties.
> Viet-Nam welcomes gladly the teaching born of the experience of these democratic states, all the more as it is consistent with the political humanism and the historical situation of Viet-Nam.

This quest for progress toward stability and democracy must be founded on a solid basis:

> Such a basis can only be a spiritualist one; such a line [of progress], that which the human person follows in his innermost reality as in his community life, in his transcendent vocation as in his free pursuit of intellectual, moral and spiritual perfection.
> Thus we affirm our faith in the absolute value of the human person, whose dignity antedates society and whose destiny is grander than time.
> . . . the sole legitimate end and object of the state is to protect the fundamental rights of the human person to existence and to the free development of his intellectual, moral and spiritual life.
> We affirm that democracy . . . is essentially a permanent effort to find the right political means for assuring to all citizens the right of free development and of maximum initiative, responsibility, and spiritual life.

In another speech in similar vein, the President said:

> The history of mankind offers two solutions: the capitalist solution through freedom and the Communist solution through coercion . . . Both, the free capitalist and the forced Communist, solutions have achieved great industrial progress, but both, especially the Communist solution, have inflicted great damage on man.
> Realizing this fact, the most advanced elements of mankind are seeking a third solution capable of quickly achieving the industrial revolution without the evil consequences of the two above.

Here the President was somewhat more specific about the "third solution":

> Personalism, Community Work [referred to elsewhere as "community development"] and collective social advancement represent the effort of the advanced elements of the Republic of Viet Nam in this direction.[30]

President Ngo has said that the attainment of these goals will require austerity, community discipline, the sacrifice of "petty interest" and the abandonment of "a desire for excessive enjoyment" but, on the other hand, the very nature of such goals "limits the exigencies of an excessively rigid discipline. This limit is based upon active respect for the human being within the scope of community interests. . . ."[31]

Western and Eastern Values

Personalism was first presented to the general Vietnamese public by the National Cultural Congress of February, 1957, which was attended largely by officials and political figures and reported widely in the press. Ngo Dinh Nhu delivered a key speech in the one-week program, tracing the historical efforts of the Vietnamese to develop an "authentic culture." He went back to the advent of European colonialism and discussed the Asian reaction of analyzing "the causes of their inferiority" and making "a veritable 'census' of their spiritual and moral values . . . considered up to that time immutable." As they struggled for independence, Asians "sought to acquire that which appeared to be the basis of the western nations' power," namely, their science and modern technique, while safeguarding their traditional values. This movement was continuing and would have produced better results if its leaders had possessed "a solid criterion" to guide them in distinguishing "real from false values."

Nhu believed "spirit," not "technique," had given the West supremacy over Asia. European culture had sprung from the "Evangelical spirit," an "instrument to appreciate human values," and "mathematical thought and the Greek dialectic" which had served as means of dominating nature. Turning to Asian cultures, Nhu said that "the principles of respect for the human person are found in the Rig Veda, the Upanishads, in Mencius and in the popular tradition of Vietnam." Thus, he concluded, "the criterion sought for our national culture is none other than the human person, living in community."[32] The Congress resolved to "create a National Cultural Association to defend and illustrate the national culture . . ." and Ngo Dinh Nhu became chairman of the preparatory committee.

Nhu presented a more detailed analysis of the personalist elements in Asian traditional thought in a 1959 speech. He maintained that the doctrines principally determinant on Asian civilization has been Hinduism, Buddhism, Confucianism, and the Taoism of Lao-tse. However, he emphasized as essentially personalist ideas the following, not all of which had ranked in the "most influential" category: the belief in a transcendental Absolute or Being and its residence within the heart of man, as taught by the Indian Rig Veda; the compassion and human tenderness taught by Buddhism; the development of later "heretical" Buddhism, away from the original agnostic phenomenism in which Nirvana represented extinction of the individual, toward "a kind of affective theism" involving prayer to a transcendental God and a paradise in which the enlightened "enjoy a blissful vision without losing their personalities"; the humanity of Confucius who put man, endowed with spiritual qualities, "at the base of the universal order"; and finally Mo-ti's doctrine of universal love and his description of an omnipresent, all powerful, personal God.[33]

Nhu and the President have both cited also the equality of men as an old Asian personalist value dating from the opposition of Buddhism to the Indian caste system. Ngo Dinh Diem has also spoken of the traditional notion of "freedom born of the spontaneous emergence of the Taoist being."[34]

Nhu here stated his belief in certain "permanent and universal values" contained in these traditional systems along with other values which had disappeared. This position on values is similar to Mounier's, which holds that personalist values have existed through time because they are genuine responses to human needs which have varied little between historical periods and civilizations. Thus Mounier believed that much of the ethics of such Asian philosophies as Confucianism and Buddhism would always remain valid.

The difficulty in trying to draw a distinction between "Eastern" and "Western" values, in view of the historical-cultural interflow between East and West and the independent or parallel existence of such values in both areas has been discussed by Nguyen Huy Bao, Dean of the Faculty of Letters of the University of Saigon. He has offered comparative groups of Eastern and Western values which agree basically with Nhu's description given above.[35]

The problem of developing a national cultural system was described by President Ngo during his state visit to India in November, 1957. He attempted to outline the direction of Vietnamese thought toward the "search for an appropriate formula from among those presented by various ideologies which today are disputing the hegemony of the world." These questions were relevant to the problem:

> Does not the force of western technique, which some of us despise, while others admire without reservation, contain a creative spirit which justifies it? Likewise, does not our spiritualism, of which we are so proud, simply conceal a narrow conservatism or a form of escapism from concrete historical responsibilities? Has not Buddhist

131784

> compassion become a pretext for not practicing justice, which must
> precede all charity? And is not tolerance, which we so readily mistake
> for freedom, the result of paternalistic indulgence, [and a] lack of
> inner convictions. . . . ?

Without answers to these questions, Ngo said, Asians might get "bogged
down in a statism which is synonymous with death," or abandon themselves "to an indiscriminate cultural receptiveness, which is no less dangerous."

On the prospects for developing a Vietnamese cultural "formula,"
Ngo said: "I am convinced that with better research methods and with
the cultural means of expression endowed with insight, preciseness and
clarity, Asian genius, henceforth [oriented] toward the exploitation of
nature for the service of Man, and no longer toward the identification
of Man with nature, will find in its western-enriched cultural heritage
the solution of its problems."[36]

UNOFFICIAL FORMULATIONS OF VIETNAMESE PERSONALISM

There is no systematic, "official" formulation of personalism for the
general public, although a book[37] recently published by the League of
National Revolutionary Civil Servants presents material taught in the
Vinh Long Personalism Training Center, said to have been edited by the
Can Lao party (both discussed below).

This book of abridged lectures by three Dominican fathers presents a
theistic natural-law philosophy which draws heavily on Greek and particularly European sources including Aquinas and papal encyclicals
such as *Rerum Novarum* and *Quadragesimo Anno*. Asian traditions are
hardly mentioned and Asian philosophies such as Confucianism, Buddhism, and Taoism are not cited. A preface by Interior Secretary Lam
Le Trinh states that personalism has a value "not reciprocally related to
religion" which every reader is duty-bound to try to grasp. The book,
while not an argument for Christianity, presents a philosophical picture
of man, free will, conscience, the soul, the ultimate value (finding God),
the family, society, and human rights which is essentially Thomist.
(Thomism, despite its *de facto* connection with Catholicism, is not a
part of the Catholic faith.)[38] It differs from the private monographs
discussed below in that it does not deal with Maritain, Mounier, and the
other very modern personalists usually cited, and it does not suggest
specific social and economic reforms as do some of the monographs.

Personalism has been discussed, often in fragmentary fashion, in
speeches by political leaders, in government publications including *Vietnam Press* news bulletins, in pamphlets and booklets of the Information

Department and the Presidency's Press Bureau, and in the officially supported newspapers. The proceedings of the National Cultural Congress of 1957 have been published in book form. In May, 1958 the Tinh Viet literary group announced two new prizes for a novel and an essay devoted to the "primacy of the Mind over the Body and upholding the values of the Human Person."[39] Bui Tuan's *Personalism, Basis of Reconstruction*[40] won second prize in the essay division of the revived annual literary competition in 1958.

Tuan's is one of the privately published works on personalism[41] which are limited to their authors' private views and have no official endorsement. When Ngo Dinh Nhu was once asked by an information official about the adequacy of two of these books, he replied that they contained contradictions and inaccuracies, and that "special study periods" were necessary to clarify personalist conceptions. Despite this and the variations between them, however, these monographs do provide some additional information on the specifically Vietnamese version of personalist doctrine and on social reform proposals circulating to an unknown extent among personalists and government leaders.

One writer, for example, follows the French personalist view that all philosophical investigation of a humanist bent from Plato, Aristotle, and Confucius to the present is a part of the personalist tradition. He lists among modern contributors to personalist thought many of those cited by the French Catholic school, including Bergson and Gabriel Marcel. In mentioning German and British personalists he even includes novelist Graham Greene.

This writer cites the Confucian view that man's nature is basically good, not evil, and continues:

> Confucianism emphasizes and elevates the *Nhan* [man] and stresses love as the essential part of human conduct. Confucius says: . . . "Natural virtue resides in Man" and . . . "Heaven gives spirit and spirit makes man." Confucius thus acknowledged the Personalist conception of man issuing from that Heavenly decree.

Emphasizing the importance of man in the universe, the writer quotes the Confucian saying that "The principle of the Tao [the Way] is not far from man, if it is the true Tao." He also links with personalism the Confucian notion of "self-improvement" and the idea developed further by Mencius that a good environment must be provided man to permit the ripening of virtue in him. He notes also that "the 'Three Virtues' of Buddhism [charity, intelligence, courage] come within the personalist conception. . ."[42]

Some Vietnamese personalists have carried their emphasis on Asian traditional sources of personalist thought to considerable lengths. A

Catholic priest is reported to have told the National Cultural Congress in 1957, "I believe that in Vietnamese culture there already is a store of Personalism and that we do not need to borrow, to seek from afar. Let us return to . . . the noble culture of Viet-Nam."[43] He also said, "There are people who believe that spiritualism is particular to Catholicism. But I believe one should not be concerned about [this] because spiritualism belongs to all, to man who believes there is a soul, who believes that man has not only a material aspect but also a spiritual nature and considers the latter primary. . ."[44]

A spirit of religious tolerance bordering on eclecticism is found in some of these statements. Professor Le Huu Muc told the National Cultural Congress, "Confucianism, Buddhism, Taoism, Catholicism, all these spiritual [sic] systems not only trace for man a suitable philosophy of life, but also are very effective means of opposing Communism and are deep and abundant sources of inspiration for all branches of the arts and letters."[45]

The roles of government and religion are put in a neo-Thomist perspective in the following passages of a monograph: ". . . the government shall observe the principle of true freedom of religion and shall help religion to expand and to enable it to lead man to perfection."[46]

> . . . Religon is outside and above politics. It is outside in the sense that it ordinarily does not enter politics. It is above, because religion resolves problems fundamental to the origin and end of man . . . politics must support the material conditions for the existence of religion and must allow decisions, intervention and the opposition of religion in questions related to the transcendental values of man and society.[47]

An antagonism toward both the power blocs is sometimes found in these writings:

> Thus facing a bloc of 600 million Communist Chinese plotting against the South to assimilate our people, and before the strong expansion of the capitalist countries using economic means to control small countries which have just obtained independence, we have only one way to survive and resist being swallowed by the two politico-economic blocs. That is the way of building Personalism on a basis of spiritualism.[48]

Another writer says:

> The capitalist and Communist systems of the present are dividing the world into two parts. The capitalist side respects man but only men of wealth or nobility . . . The Communists only' "respect" the proletarian and see him as a tool, a machine, a creature.
> . . . The Personalist society of tomorrow will be a truly democratic society; there will not be the tyranny of wealth and nobility nor the dictatorship of the proletariat . . . in it, men will not be differentiated as rich or poor nor by their skin color nor beliefs, and each will have the right to live a life conforming to his own material and spiritual values.[49]

Some of the personalist writers describe economic policies of a future personalist society similar to those in French MRP doctrine, and stress a semi-socialist pattern of welfare and social security. One writer favors government ownership of electric power and water facilities and government rationalization of economic processes to the extent of

> directing or guiding production and distribution to avoid speculation and exploitation of the people and the upsetting of the market. It will let the people buy for very reasonable prices . . .
> . . . Government will fix prices of essential goods and the profit level of business enterprises.
> . . . Government [will] not compete with private individuals but assist and harmonize the activities of individuals.

Father Tran Huu Thanh and others divide the economy into three sectors receiving varying degrees of government supervision. The production of subsistence goods (food, clothing, petroleum, etc.) is closely regulated by the government to provide for sufficient quantity, transportation to all areas, and fair prices. In the production and distribution of amenities ("bicycles, watches, good quality materials for clothing, etc."), the government allows more private competition but still exercises direct control to alleviate shortages and protect local industry from foreign competition. The third sector satisfies "developmental" or "spiritual and aesthetic" needs and includes such production as "special inventions, precious books and journals, and works of art." Here there is no government regulation but government does award prizes to stimulate production.[50]

Father Thanh defends the principle of private property as modified by the "three principles of sharing" (tam dong). These stipulate that workers and farmers shall share with owners in management and in the division of profits. The former, who have "mixed their sweat and tears with the owner's capital" have a right to live permanently on the land they have tilled or to work permanently in the factory or shop of their employment. Their children in turn retain a priority of access to these benefits.

Workers and farmers also have a right to participate in all substantive policy decisions of management. The profit-sharing system does not attempt "to level income or profit as in the Communist vision, because the rights of each person are different." However, the owner should retain only a certain share of the "huge sums" comprising profits and use the rest for such workers' benefits as scholarships for their children, schools, hospitals, clinics, and useful entertainment.

Big businesses are to be nationalized if this is necessary to prevent "abuses and exploitation" and the socialization process follows the "three principles of sharing."[51]

Producers' and consumers' cooperatives are described as the mainstay of the future personalist economy. They benefit producers and consumers by reducing the profits of middlemen and moneylenders. Private merchants still operate but their economic returns are scaled down to approximate those of government employees.[52]

There is to be a general mechanization of small-scale as well as large-scale production and a dispersal of production to allow workers to live in their original villages instead of being concentrated in distant cities. Cooperatives distribute materials to these scattered production units and market their finished products. The family regime will characterize the small units; parents will thus be able to take better care of their children and Vietnamese society will preserve its customs against the forces of too-rapid change.[53]

These personalist monographs frequently mention the universal scope of the desired personalist revolution. One of them says, "The United Nations is the existing organ urging all countries and peoples to a *world-wide Personalist* revolution . . . it is certain that someday all humanity will live in an international Personalist society."[54]

PERSONALIST POLICIES AND PROGRAMS

Land Development and the Basic-Property Policy

Certain government programs have been cited specifically by Ngo Dinh Diem as directed toward personalist goals. These are, first of all, the land programs including refugee settlement, land reform, and land development. Here the President has expressed the government's desire that each citizen have "the opportunity to become the owner of his (own) basic amount of property," a house and a piece of land, his concrete guarantees of a free life. "Every farmer without land, every town-dweller, every worker's family can have his basic property."[55]

In an earlier speech Ngo Dinh Nhu stressed the basic piece of property idea as integral to a "new conception of private ownership" which contributes to the material basis for the spiritual mission of personalism. Individual ownership of houses on tracts of from one to three hectares (2½ to 7½ acres) yielding rice or other crops would offer an economic guarantee which Nhu considers essential for the citizen's independence of spirit, and would provide subsistence for urban workers in case of unemployment. The concept contributes significantly to Nhu's hopes for a general increase in productivity per family that would result in bigger tax revenues and private investment funds to be channeled into the industrialization program. "If every citizen, apart from his work in a public or private office, has a family which makes another [income from such a piece of property], then they add up their two [incomes] and naturally they will be able to pay the tax . . . and . . . use the remaining sum to participate with the government in building industries."[56] Finally, this program has an additional potential purpose: it would provide for the rapid absorption of the great wave of refugees which Nhu expects would rush from North Vietnam to the South in the event of national reunification. Those settled on such units of basic property could accommodate refugee individuals or families temporarily until permanent arrangements could be made for their welfare.

This basic-property policy is being carried out by both the regular land reform program and the land resettlement programs sending groups of settlers to pioneer farm communities in such areas as the highlands of Central Vietnam. (These programs are described in chapter 7.)

The more recent "agroville" program bears similarities to the highlands resettlement plan. The government has designated two sites in each of the 12 southwestern provinces for dramatic transformation from isolated, relatively uncultivated back-country areas often "infested with pirates and rebels" into model communities with electricity and street lighting, good road connections to the outside system, canals, markets, schools, hospitals or infirmaries, maternity clinics, community halls, farmers' association halls, horticultural nurseries, etc. Farmers moving into an agroville from the surrounding area continue to cultivate their original ricefields but are given garden plots in the agroville, together with house plans and building materials. Similarly, government loans enable the construction of commercial shops around the market. The first agroville, completed in March, 1960, included 750 houses.[57]

There are other major goals served by the agroville program besides the basic-property aim, including combatting Communist infiltration and increasing agricultural productivity in these sparsely populated areas. But preventing the formation of a socially unstable proletariat is a real concern and the President has spoken of the land resettlement program, for example, in terms of "deproletarianization."[58]

Ngo Dinh Diem has stressed the role of such agencies and programs as "Agricultural Credit, Cooperatives, the Farmers' Union and Community Development"[59] in the "consolidation and extension of this basic property." The community-development program aims to raise living standards both in rural areas and crowded urban areas[60] by pooling the efforts of the government with those of the people who furnish free labor on local projects. On the bigger rural projects, several thousand people work for one or more days on a local canal, dike, road, school building, etc.[61] The Cong Hoa [Republican] Youth Movement, a government mass organization, has furnished much of the labor for such projects and the agrovilles. Cong Hoa Youth from eight provinces helped construct the Mo Cay Agroville in Kien Hoa Province, for example.[62] (Unfortunately, local officials often have pushed these "voluntary" work forces over-zealously to complete construction ahead of schedule, have kept them on some projects too long at one stint, and have failed to provide adequate food and housing for them. Many farmers dislike moving from their original homes and some have had to walk long distances—up to 12 kilometers—from their agrovilles to reach their rice fields. Consequently, the agroville program has aroused the hostility of peasants in some areas.)

The Can-Lao Party

As noted earlier, Ngo Dinh Nhu has been particularly influential in the personalist movement since his contact with French personalism in the 1930's. After completing his studies at the Ecole des Chartes, Nhu returned to Vietnam as a chief librarian. He did research for a history of Vietnam but his materials were destroyed during the war with the Viet Minh. He believed the Vietnamese nationalists working for independence lacked both political knowledge and doctrine and were just practicing "political handicrafts." At that early date, it is said, he believed personalism should become the philosophical basis of the Vietnamese revolution.

In about 1948, Nhu met with the *Tinh-Than* [Spirit] group to popularize his theories. In 1953 and 1954 he was the leader of the *Xa-Hoi* [Society] group. In 1954, Nhu organized the *Can-Lao Nhan-Vi Cach-Mang Dang*, literally, the Personalist Revolutionary Labor Party but often called in English the Revolutionary Workers' Party for Human Dignity. It influenced labor through the related Vietnam Confederation of Christian Workers (incidentally, the Vietnamese title does not include the word "Christian") and there is some similarity here to the French MRP's relationship to the *Confédération française des travailleurs chrétiens* (CFTC).

The *Can-Lao*, as it is popularly called, is a powerful elite political party. Although it has been represented in seats on the extreme left in the National Assembly, its general membership and activities are secret. The members are commonly believed to belong to other political parties also and to dominate them. The intimate relationship of this party with the government is indicated by certain special investigative functions it possesses, enabled by the anonymity of its membership. Members are thus in an advantageous position to pick up reports of malfeasance, corruption and Communist infiltration which otherwise might not reach the government because of the average citizen's fear of reprisals from colleagues or superiors. The party then sends a commission to investigate the allegations and "if these are proved to be well founded, it takes action to secure the arrest and trial of the guilty persons."[63]

The Personalism Training Center

Another of the President's brothers, Bishop Ngo Dinh Thuc, set up an experimental personalism course in October, 1956 at Vinh Long. It was considered so successful that a national "Personalism Training Center" was established there. Courses now are held throughout the year for civil servants, school teachers, political party members, etc. Government officials receive leaves of absence with pay to take the course. By May, 1960, 3,000 persons in 26 classes had completed the training.[64]

The original faculty of five was composed of Catholic priests and the original director, Father Tran Muc Dich, was also responsible for the academic training of officer candidates at the Dalat military academy. During his absence, Father Phero Nguyen Tu, a secular priest who had been very active in organizing the center, was to take charge. He had studied in Rome for five years and then studied under the French personalist Jacques Paliard at the University of Aix-en-Provence for two years. Connected with the center is a community information bureau "where the people can . . . inquire about anything . . . from legal procedures to agricultural methods . . . social welfare programs or educational curricula and [the] military draft. Returned civil servants are volunteering their time to serve as personnel for the (bureau)."[65]

Spread of Personalism Through Political Action and Legislation

The doctrine of personalism is spread in the countryside by "Civil Action" teams which work for a few weeks each in villages to restore basic public services. Following the National Cultural Congress in Saigon, various personalism study-groups were organized in the provinces.[66] Personalism was also honored by a new postage stamp released on Constitution Day (October 26), 1958.[67] Support of the powerful government political groups long has been pledged to personalism.

The January 1956 manifesto of the National Revolutionary Movement (NRM) assigned to personalism a primary role in the revolution.[68] Political groups' statements (and particularly resolutions of support for the President) make references to personalism which often are so brief as to suggest mere political slogans. More substantial support for the doctrine was reported, however, in an April, 1958 announcement of goals of the NRM's refugee centers program. One was "propagation of the personalist doctrine . . . with a keen interest in putting it into effect."[69] More recently, the majority group in the National Assembly has been designated the "Personalist Bloc."

The most controversial of the new legislative measures dedicated to personalism has been Mme Ngo Dinh Nhu's "Family Bill," promulgated in January, 1959, which spells out women's rights to an extent unprecedented in Asian or even western societies. The law, containing 134 articles regulating the status of the family, aroused opposition in the Assembly and among elements of the public chiefly for its prohibition of divorce except under very unusual circumstances. In its place it substitutes a "physical separation." This provision enables an incompatible husband and wife to live apart, but does not permit a legal dissolution of their marriage, nor an opportunity to remarry. A suit for "physical separation" may be filed on three grounds: adultery,[70] cruelty and serious physical maltreatment, or grave mental and psychological abuses. A temporary decree may be granted after one hearing upon the failure of an attempted reconciliation, but a final decree is not awarded until three such reconciliations have failed in the course of one year. In exceptionally unhappy cases a legal divorce may be awarded, but only after President Ngo himself has consulted with the judges of two courts having jurisdiction, the couple's family heads, and the couple themselves.[71] Annulment is possible in a number of cases. It may be granted, for example, within a year of the discovery that a condition of "permanent impotence" had existed prior to the marriage.

The law outlaws polygamy and concubinage and gives persons found in these relations two months to legalize or dissolve them; it enables a husband or wife to forbid the spouse from "keeping a too-close relationship with any designated person of the opposite sex whom he or she regards as harmful to the marriage," with fines and imprisonment for non-compliance. Another controversial provision prevents a mother from suing the father of her illegitimate child for support if he is already married to another woman. The law also sets minimum marriageable ages at 18 for men and 15 for women, requires the consent of both partners to a betrothal, permits a wife to work, and permits her to refuse to live with her husband's parents if the couple has sufficient means to set up their own household. The "spirit of personalism . . . constitutes the leading thought of the 'Family Bill'," according to the joint committee reporting it to the Assembly in December, 1957.[72] The delay in the Assembly's passage of it until May, 1958 was marked by "lengthy and passionate debate," at least on the divorce ban. Mme Nhu's original version of the bill apparently called for unequivocal prohibition of divorce until the draft version was amended in the Assembly.[73]

After the bill was passed, Mme Nhu commented that the Vietnamese wife, no longer exposed to unfair competition from other wives and concubines in the family and no longer vulnerable to persecution by her husband, would now be able to "develop her whole personality fully."[74] In an earlier defense of "physical separation," she said it "would preserve the spouses from excesses, [and] protect society against structural disintegration." Henceforth married couples would be protected by "the knowledge that their union will be [for] forever. They will choose their partner for a lifetime and no longer only for a season . . ."[75]

The full impact of the Family Law on Vietnamese society remains to be seen, but two and a half months after it went into effect the officially-subsidized *Times of Vietnam* reported that it had already brought Vietnamese women to a new consciousness of their rights under an older law against wife-beating. Previously this law had gone largely unenforced, because even if a husband were punished for such an act he could too easily take revenge on his wife:

> On [his] return from jail it was easy to provoke the disobedience of his wife and thereafter legally renounce her, . . . take a concubine, or . . . simply leave the family home. Since the law no longer protects him in this revenge, it appears the men who beat their wives are suddenly being brought into the court in significant numbers . . .

The Justice Department was reported to be receiving many complaints and inquiries about the application of the new law, many of them in unsatisfactory legal form, so it set up a consultation office in Saigon to assist women whose problems might fall within the provisions of the law, but who could not afford legal fees.[76]

Mme Nhu has led other family-protection efforts, including the founding of a Social Solidarity Movement. She obtained the support of such groups as the Congress of Women Civil Servants and the National Revolutionary Civil Servants League in a plan to set up committees in all rural areas. The movement is voluntary and financed by women's contributions, enough of which were received to build a kindergarten at Dalat in November, 1958.[77] Programs of the Directorate-General of Social Action to the Presidency appear to be closely related to those organized by Mme Nhu: it has attempted to establish a system of "inter-family assistance" and other measures which also would be carried out through provincial and village committees. The stated goal of these programs is "a new style of living for each family and individual in accordance with the personalist teachings."[78]

The *lien-gia* or combined-family protection unit system has been set up in Vietnam by the Ngo government, and serves the inter-family assistance program.[79] This organization of neighborhoods into basic units of five to twenty households resembles the traditional systems of China and Japan, and interestingly enough, the present-day mutual-aid family societies in France. It also resembles faintly the system of neighborhood cell organizations of Communist China and North Vietnam. They are used extensively in these Communist countries for political purposes, and in the Republic of Vietnam they have an apparently similar range of functions, among which public security functions are paramount.

Other family-protection measures include a law of July, 1958 that set up juvenile courts with jurisdiction over delinquents under 18 (unless they have older accomplices). Children as young as 13 may be dealt with under the ordinary penal code, but a variety of alternatives are possible, including commitment to parents, guardian, or welfare agency. Youthful defendants must have counsel who may be appointed by the bar if necessary. The name of a convicted child must not be published by the press.[80]

Under Vietnam's labor code workers are unusually well protected from certain occupational hazards. Employers are responsible for all accidents on the job, even if they are due to the "worker's clumsiness or mistake," and even for traffic accidents affecting workers going to or from work.[81]

Personalism in Education and Indoctrination Programs

Vietnamese education is undergoing revision and synthesis to safeguard its "national character" and "enrich our patrimony by genuine values from Occidental civilizations," according to the Education Secretary, Tran Huu The. Launching the Preparatory Commission for Revision of the Secondary Education Program in April, 1958, he acknowledged that while some improvements had been made since 1949, "now it is high time for us to consider basic principles for a wholesale reform of the system."[82] A new curriculum was inaugurated in both government and private high schools in October, 1958.[83] The new policy has been called "personalistic, nationalistic, and scientific." To achieve the "personalistic" aim, a *Times of Vietnam* editorial said, education must "make our students think for themselves."[84] Secretary The later amplified the personalist aim by stressing "the necessity for safeguarding the 'humanist trend' which, through the ages, has continuously inspired all educators—from Confucius to Montaigne and Rousseau . . ."[85]

In line with the nationalist aim of the new education, Secretary The said Vietnamese language and literature should be emphasized in the program, and should include the Chinese characters where necessary to facilitate the study of the national romanized language.[86] (This does not indicate any reduction of emphasis on western languages, however, as can be seen in Ngo's speeches in India and Seoul, wherein he stressed the value of such languages as "remarkable tools for analysis and abstraction.")[87]

Five leading personalist scholars are members of the Faculty of Letters of the University of Saigon. No courses are devoted to personalism as such, but these professors are free to bring personalist ideas into discussions of philosophy and related subjects. They are Nguyen Huy Bao, Dean of the Faculty of Letters, Nguyen Dang Thuc and Catholic priests Buu Duong (who also teaches at the University of Hue), Nguyen Van Thich, and M. Cras (a Frenchman).

The Vietnamese government's extensive anti-Communist indoctrination program which began in 1955 features monthly meetings of government and military personnel, various types of workers, village groups, etc. Communist ideology is attacked and personal hardships under the Viet Minh are described by group members and outside speakers. A training document says:

> "This campaign has two aspects: . . . it denounces the false ideology of the Communists . . . [and] it propagates the 'personalist' doctrine . . . We are endeavoring to oppose that degenerate Marxist ideology with a superior philosophy founded on the spiritual conception of man in the community . . . Collective materialism is inadequate for these purposes for it reduces man to a creature of material ends and motives. To raise the standard of living, as desirable and necessary as it is, is neither a total answer to the basic needs and aspirations of man nor a suitable answer to Communism."[88]

Personalism is evidently one of the components of the training given political prisoners (surrendered and captured Communist personnel and other persons suspected of having Communist sympathies) in the government's "political reeducation centers" as well.[89]

PERSONALISM AND THE VIETNAMESE "HISTORICAL MISSION"

Top government leaders have referred to a historical mission for Vietnam in such terms as the following statement by Ngo Dinh Nhu: "The enormous difficulties Vietnam faces constitute our destiny . . . It will be a great honor for our generation if we know how to make our culture 'ferment' by the 'leaven' of the human person which will enrich it in all aspects without pushing it toward extremist solutions of the right or left."[90] Although it has been only fragmentarily described, this mission evidently has two aspects: (1) propagation of personalist thought within Vietnam, one hoped-for result being the eventual downfall of the North Vietnam Communist regime; and (2) development of a personalism-oriented bloc of countries in Southeast Asia, under at least moral guidance from Vietnam, which could ultimately contribute to the collapse of Communist movements there, as well as to progress toward other personalist goals of economic and spiritual development.

CONCLUSION

The Morality and Confucian Campaigns in Political Perspective

The phenomenon of campaigns for spiritual as well as social renovation is not unusual in newly independent countries. There was such a campaign in Vietnam in the fifteenth century: "In keeping with the spirit of national renovation generated during the war against the Chinese, [Emperor Le Loi] imposed a strictly puritanical regime on his country in order to speed up the process of reconstruction. Under his penal code even laziness and gambling became major crimes."[91] More recently, the Viet Minh conducted a morality campaign in North Vietnam in late 1945.

To a Westerner there is much that seems coercive and arbitrary in the Ngo government's anti-vice and anti-Communist propaganda campaigns, but they must be considered in their historical context. The earlier campaigns were launched in the government's desperate need for popular support of its anti-Communist position in the July, 1956 national elections stipulated under the Geneva agreements, elections which would determine whether it could prevail against the powerful northern Communist regime in the ruling of the whole country. The most serious problem was the low educational level of much of the population at whom the government had to direct its campaigns. More important, the stress of continuous political and security problems over the years had dazed and disillusioned the people and left many of them an easy prey for the Communist propaganda agents hard at work among them. Later, when national stability permitted, large-scale educational programs including civic training were intensified, but the propaganda campaigns preceding the personalism campaign were conceived essentially as emergency measures.

How does Confucianism fit into the national reconstruction effort? The writer recalls the reaction of a Saigon student leader (recently arrived from Hanoi) to a similar question in 1956. He shrugged and replied that Confucianism had been a major factor in the Chinese Nationalist Government's defeat by the Communists in 1949. Many of the modern generation have shared this attitude, as is acknowledged in the Confucian Association's manifesto described above. This may have been the reason for the government's earlier emphasis on certain traditional values without reference to them as Confucian (as in a Ngo speech cited above).

The present policy of forthright espousal of Confucianism does not represent an unqualified endorsement, however. Dean Nguyen Huy Bao has commented that along with its positive contributions, Confucianism includes many ideas antagonistic to modern conceptions of the nation-state and economic progress. Therefore, a personalist view of the citizen and a modern view of the state are more appropriate than the old "family individualism" with its sentiment of "Perish the nation so long as my family prospers."[92] However, the government's enthusiasm for Confucianism appears to embrace publicly only selected elements—the broad humanist ethos and the Confucian masculine virtues discussed above. Significantly, there is little mention of the subordinate moral rank of the younger to the elder and of woman to man, as the latter was traditionally expressed in the three deferential relationships [tam tong] of the woman, and the feminine "four virtues" [tu duc] which further delineate the subordinate and passive aspects of her role.

Another modern note in this revival of Confucianism relates to the Confucian Association's statement cited above, that the doctrine is appropriate to modern living because it teaches "that people must change according to the nature of their era to conform to the laws of evolution of human society." This idea is essentially incompatible with the Confucian tradition and recalls attempts by certain Chinese scholars from the nineteenth century onward to "reinterpret" the Confucian texts and thus revise drastically the doctrine to make it compatible with Western science and cultural values related to the concept of progress.

Problems of Reconciling Eastern and Western Values

One of the most interesting aspects of Vietnamese personalism is the attempted linkage of Western and Asian traditional concepts of a transcendental Being. French Catholic personalism has obviously determined much of the Ngos' philosophical groundwork for this. Nhu's analysis of those Asian beliefs contributing most directly to this personalist concept clearly centers around spiritual, theistic concepts which are compatible with Christianity. His description of the *personal* quality of the *t'ien* [God or Heaven] of Mo-ti illustrates an interpretation which would be challenged by many scholars of Chinese philosophy.

Likewise, both Ngo Dinh Nhu and the President see in Confucianism a traditional sanction for belief in the God of Christianity, or at least in a similar deity. For example, President Ngo's Confucian message of October, 1959 included this passage:

> Confucianism has already taught our fathers respect for the Creator and obedience to His will as a criterion of moral behavior: 'When one ignores God's will, one is not a superior man,' said Confucius.
> Faith in the Almighty advocated in Confucianism leads to another faith: faith in the sacred worth of the spirit of man . . .
> [According to this faith], we ought to show respect to the Almighty and our ancestors on the one hand, and we must show faithfulness, loyalty and justice to our fellow countrymen.

This reference to the existence of a Supreme Being in Confucian dogma might be said to conflict with much that has been said about its rationalistic, secular, man-centered, and essentially agnostic character. Ngo Dinh Diem does reveal his own theological view in his interpretation, but there is considerable evidence to support the notion that theistic conceptions did exist in at least the older Confucian teachings.[93] One priest on the faculty of the University of Saigon stresses the compatibility of Confucianism with personalism, and evidently believes that a general study of Confucianism would be conducive to a wider acceptance of Christianity in Vietnam. (In this view he appears to agree with the writings of the Chinese Catholic, Lou Tseng-tsiang.)

To some extent this sort of attitude is a commentary on the weakened influence of Buddhism in Vietnam today compared with its vigor in neighboring Southeast Asian countries. The governments of Thailand and Burma, for example, have enjoyed effective Buddhist support for their cultural and anti-Communist propaganda. Even if they had desired it, the Ngo brothers would have sought in vain for such support from the adherents of Vietnam's Mahayana Buddhism, which has been thoroughly diluted by mythology, animism, Taoism, and Confucianism.[94]

Will this fundamental compatibility of Vietnamese personalism with the general mood of Christian transcendentalism alienate the non-Catholic Vietnamese who constitute over 90 per cent[95] of the population? President Ngo does extend a certain amount of overt support to Christianity. In his annual Christmas message of 1959, for example, he said:

> . . . it is essential for us to remember the vital Message which Jesus Christ brought to us two thousand years ago: only in the service of justice and charity can science be of true value to civilization, and can man achieve peace in his heart and throughout the world.

Perhaps the closest President Ngo has come to a public endorsement of Christianity came in the next passage. Speaking of Vietnamese living under the tyranny of the North Vietnam government and the hopes they have in their southern compatriots, the President said: "It is by observing the Evangelical Message in our private and public lives that we will be able, to some extent, to justify this confidence."[96]

However, such statements should not be construed to mean that the Ngos and their top-echelon political leaders intend to use personalism to proselytize the Vietnamese nation for Christianity. Ngo Dinh Diem has not shown any inclination towards a facile, dogmatic application of his personal religious views to his role as President. There has been some political confrontation of Catholics and Buddhists on such occasions as the Assembly debate on the term for "the Almighty" to be used in the Constitution, and a satisfactory solution was reached.[97] European personalist movements, incidentally, have usually included both Christian elements and secular, liberal intellectual, humanist elements, as in the case of *Esprit* and also the MRP. These movements have not demanded that all their collaborators embrace Christianity, and the Vietnamese movement follows the same pattern.

Such collaboration inevitably raises the question of a possible threat to Catholic orthodoxy. In 1953 a commentator noted on developments in France that "Recently . . . there have been some hints of Vatican pressure against those Christian Democrats who have been 'seeking to build a bridge between the Church and the modern world,' and who have been trying to cooperate with non-Catholic democratic groups."[98]

Father Nguyen Van Tu of the Vinh Long Personalism Training Center was recently asked about possible risks in "pan-religionism exploited for unity in emergency," and he answered as follows:

> Our [trainee] group is pluralist here because ours is a pluralistic land—Buddhists, Confucians, Christians, etc., with the Christians in a decided minority. Otherwise it would not be a representative [assemblage] . . . The breadth of Catholicism as a *culture* (bridging continents and centuries) does not jeopardize its doctrinal core. Only within this latter is there any possibility of making the mistake of syncretism—and the students and I will assure you that we have neither the occasion nor the desire to intrude here.[99]

In discussing the contemporary confrontation of Western Christian and Asian traditional values, Vietnamese writers point proudly to the historical syntheses their people have made of the older, originally antagonistic philosophies such as Confucianism and Buddhism.[100] In this connection, a leading Vietnamese philosopher has cited the Indian modernist of the 17th-18th centuries, Rammohun Roy, as having first "synthesized Christianity with Upanishad philosophy."[101] In his admiration, however, the Vietnamese exaggerates the accomplishment: Roy omitted Christian doctrine and combined only Christian ethics in his system.[102]

Any discussion of the present Vietnamese interest in synthesizing Western and Eastern cultural values must include mention of the Cao Dai eclectic religious movement launched in the 1920's. Its adherents consider its doctrine to be a revitalized form of Buddhism, but it includes elements of Confucianism, Taoism, spirit cults, and Christianity as well, and has a hierarchy reminiscent of the Catholic Papacy. Its saints and leading spirits include Victor Hugo, Lao-tse, Joan of Arc, Confucius, La Rochefoucauld, Saint Bernard, the prophet Malachi, and Jesus Christ. Cao Daiism holds that each of these various religions, aspects of one religious spirit, was given originally to one of the various races scattered over the earth. However, with the development of science and the great expansion of civilization, the Cao Dai [the Almighty, or "Great On-High"] communicated to founder Ngo Van Chieu, his followers believe, the desire to end this separation and reunite the branches of the faith. Some of this communication was made through a planchette-like instrument. Vietnamese personalists consider Can Daiism an unsophisticated melange, but both movements reflect the age-old Vietnamese interest in reconciling traditional thought with vital imported religious and philosophical ideas.

Little information is available concerning the possible effectiveness of personalism in the government's anti-Communist indoctrination programs. Incidentally, Viet Minh poets Xuan Dieu and Cu Huy Can were enthralled for a time during their lycée days in Hue with Mounier's writings. Can apparently had the deeper appreciation of personalism after being attracted to it in reaction against the oppression of the individual by the traditional family system and the rigid Confucianism of the day.[103] However, neither of them embraced the Catholic doctrine underlying Mounier's philosophy and both eventually switched loyalties to Communism.

Prospects for Public Acceptance of Personalism

The extent to which the Vietnamese people have accepted personalism by this time is difficult to determine, although personalist writers customarily say that the foundation has been laid for the movement. Many references to personalism in official statements have sounded so glib as to give the impression that they were included merely as concessions to current political fashion. While there is no evidence of any great degree of popular understanding or approval of personalism, it must be remembered that most of the direct efforts to propagate it have been directed at political leaders and civil servants, including schoolteachers, who are expected to pass it on to others. The personalist message which reaches the mass of the people appears to emphasize such generalities as the dignity and worth of the person, and to be designed as a psychological and spiritual antidote to the role forced on the Vietnamese by colonialism and the anti-individualistic influences of traditional Confucianism.

How closely does Vietnamese personalism accord with traditional philosophical predispositions? The doctrine as it is discussed by intellectuals in their books and journals is an abstruse one which leans heavily on Western articulation and on a conception of the dignity and value of each unique human being which originally stemmed from Christianity and subsequently penetrated Western cultural values (even as its original connection with the Christian doctrinal imperative was being attenuated). The conception did not, however, penetrate Asian cultural values to anything like the same extent. The Asian philosophical elements cited by the Ngos are generally compatible with personalism—highly selected as they are (e.g., early Confucianism and the later, "heretical" Buddhism)—but a number of them appear to serve mainly the effort to stamp personalism as harmonious with the Asian spirit rather than to further the philosophical analysis in a vital way.

Personalist Democratic Ideals and Political Realities

The government could not be expected to have developed by this time a working democracy of the order planned by Vietnamese personalists, but it is natural at this point to wonder how well the government's actions accord with its statements on personalism. In actuality there are obvious contradictions between lofty expressions of personalist ideals and some official policies. Although constitutional and statutory provisions are generally ample and, in some cases, remarkably advanced in their protection of the dignity of the citizen, the government is not yet disposed to allow interpretations of a number of them which might be theoretically more consistent with the "edification of personalist democracy" it espouses. Other writers[104] have described the strict policies affecting freedom of speech and the press, and of non-Communist political opposition in the context of the country's exceptionally burdensome security problems. The government still takes the position that the crisis situation does not permit any marked relaxation of certain strong emergency controls.

There is a moral-elitist aspect of personalism beyond the emphasis on the political and intellectual elites in efforts to propagate the doctrine. This lies in its assumption that some men are more capable than others of dealing with moral issues, and that the more morally discerning possess a natural authority over those who are less so. Thus the moral authority of the philosopher extends into politics. This is in accord with a very old Asian tradition, but it is bound to arouse antagonism and charges of hypocrisy from the secularized, modernized elements who are quick to point out the contrast between such claims of moral authority and the harshly practical politics government leaders sometimes engage in. Such criticism has been leveled at the Christian parties in Europe and, not surprisingly, at the *Can-Lao* party in Vietnam. One result of the Vietnamese application of such moral criteria to politics has been the disqualification of individuals from political participation on grounds narrower than would be generally acceptable in the West, and sometimes narrower than many Western-ized Vietnamese including Catholics find reasonable.

Personalism is conceived to be subversive of Communism. Could it conceivably become subversive in the antithetical sense of challenging the authority of the Ngo government? This question arises from the discrepancy between the personalist emphasis on the value of the human personality and the limited scope allowed in Vietnam today for the growth of the civic aspects of personality such as are developed by participation in politics and in the whole range of activities issuing from a more spontaneous clash of divergent political opinons. Such a consequence seems highly unlikely for several reasons. Vietnamese personalism predicates a fuller adjustment to one's environment through gradual, long-term, essentially spiritual growth of the person and a consequent broadening of that environment. Furthermore, be-cause personalism is a "perspective," a broad philosophical view, it does not lend itself unequivocally to the concrete demands of political programs. The Ngo government appears to have encountered some difficulty here, and any opposition group would have even more trouble in exploiting personalism politically because it is so widely identified with the Ngos.

If the government's advocacy of personalism does produce any nega-tive reactions, the worst might be cynicism from critics who are im-patient for more rapid liberalization of the regime and who could point to the distance between lofty personalist ideals and the govern-ment's sometimes illiberal practices. It must be remembered, though, that most Vietnamese have experienced only a very limited amount of political participation above the village level, and thus their conception of the goal of "personalist democracy" undoubtedly differs consider-ably from that of the urbanized intellectuals. Among the people as a whole, however, cynicism probably would not be as common as an indifference resulting from a lack of understanding of the doctrine and a general lack of interest in ideological questions. Needless to say, the government's information and propaganda organs are working hard to combat such indifference.

In the long run, personalist doctrine may not be as decisive a factor in the course of Vietnamese democratic development as the chain of everyday, pragmatic, piecemeal decisions and adjustments all govern-ments must make continuously without consistent reference to any overall ideology. There is some dissatisfaction among the Vietnamese, particularly in Saigon, over the trend of these domestic political develop-ments, and concern over the consistency of their orientation toward democratic goals. Government information media tend to emphasize the fact that Western parliamentary standards and institutions cannot be transplanted to traditional or transitional societies in any hurried, facile kind of operaion. Most observers in Vietnam as well as abroad regard as commonplaces the ideas that (1) time will be required to allow the development in Vietnam (and many other nations) of conditions which approach fulfulment of Western democratic theorists' conceptions of the socio-economic prerequisites for democracy with such features as genuine competition between two or more political parties, and (2) there is no ultimate certainty that if and when such conditions are attained, non-Western nations will necessarily find straight copies of one or another particular pattern of Western institutions ideal for their own purposes. But many of the observers who accept these premises disagree on whether the Ngo government is responding quickly enough to changing conditions which might permit increased political liberalization.[105]

Many Vietnamese officials would probably have agreed with the qualified approval of personalism given in 1957 by one of their ranking colleagues who told the writer that while personalism might well yield fundamental social results in Vietnam over a long period, immediate results were being obtained by its use in the government's more specialized anti-Communist propaganda compaigns. Today, however, the government's focus on personalism as a new national "formula" indicates its intent to give the nation something more fundamental than propaganda programs. Top leaders are convinced that something more than a pragmatic, piecemeal political approach based on a general espousal of democracy is required to cope with its extremely grave problems, including Communism.

Vietnamese personalism appears to reflect the French and Continental affinity for the more ideological approach to politics as a facet of cosmic philosophical systems or world views, in contrast to the more pragmatic approach found in the U. S. and Britain. It should be remembered here, however, that Asian tradition generally regards politics. as ideological in the sense of being one aspect of an overall cosmo-magical *Weltanschauung*. A major problem of political leaders in most non-communist Asian countries today is how to supply the theoretical linkage between their day-to-day politics, which are often conducted on a pragmatic, *ad hoc* basis, and some moral-political philosophy which they and their people revere as being relevant to politics and to life generally.

Certain U. S. political commentators are now signalling the "end of ideology" in the West. Daniel Bell contrasts the "exhausted" nineteenth century ideologies with the new mass ideologies in Asia and Africa in the following terms: the older ideologies were "universalistic, humanistic . . . fashioned by intellectuals," and their driving forces were social equality and freedom in the largest sense, while the new Asian-African ideologies are "parochial, instrumental . . . created by political leaders," and their motivating forces are the narrower ones of economic development and national power.[106]

Three points must be made concerning these statements. First, while communist ideology has become "exhausted" in the sense that it is losing its appeal for many intellectuals in the West, it still retains an important attraction for segments of the European intelligentsia. Indeed, personalism was developed in France as an antidote to the oppressive aspects of the degenerated older ideologies. These ideologies in the personalist view are mainly communism, fascism, and laissez-faire capitalism, and personalists—Vietnamese and French—are hardly ready to concede the "exhaustion" of the force of communist ideology among their peoples at this time. Second, Vietnamese personalism contrasts with these newer ideologies in its strong identification with the humanistic, universalistic strains of the older European ideologies. Here, however, a warning emerges from the history of all ideologies: to the extent that personalism, now an official doctrine in Vietnam, is transformed from a philosophy into an ideology, a system of ideas used as a political weapon (even though a weapon against great injustice), with an orthodoxy that can be challenged only at the risk of political heresy —to this extent personalism risks degenerating, as the older humanist ideologies did, into a doctrinal justification of political coercion and oppression. And finally, while some U. S. writers are theorizing about the "end of ideology," many thoughtful Americans are deeply concerned with the need for a vital, forceful democratic credo that will combat domestic political apathy and communicate an appreciation of democratic values to a number of American allies and the uncommitted peoples abroad.

Ngo Dinh Diem has said, "In this intellectual effort to stay close to a complex reality, in this revolutionary will to cover in a few years the long distance from a state of precapitalism to that of a society superior to communism, we are conscious of the immense sacrifices which we still have to make.[107] Thus the Ngo leadership, handicapped by a deadly Communist threat, shapes in its own way the political tutelage of the Vietnamese people towards the goals of national security, economic development, and democratic government, in approximately that order of priority.

[1] The term *nhan-vi* is translated into English as both "personalist" and "humanist," but the usual use of "personalist" in the official *Vietnam Press* and the officially-supported *Times of Vietnam* indicates the government's preference. The term "communal personalism" [*nhan-vi cong dong*] also is used.

The etymology of the term as written in Chinese characters yields a meaning of "human-beingness" or human category or status. (This combination of characters [Mathews 3097, 7116], cited by Vietnamese writers, does not exist in Chinese as a regular disyllabic compound.)

[2] *Major Policy Speeches by President Ngo Dinh Diem* (2nd expanded ed.; Saigon: Press Office, Presidency of the Republic of Vietnam, 1956), p. 34. The Vietnamese place the family name before the given name, but unlike the Chinese they are known commonly by the last of their given names. Great or unusually well-known men are exceptions, and in the present period Ngo Dinh Diem and Ho Chi Minh are addressed by their family names. Ngo Dinh Diem announced in 1955 that he preferred to be known as President Ngo and is so designated in this paper.

[3] Phuc Thien, *President Ngo Dinh Diem's Political Philosophy* (Saigon: Horizons, 1956), p. 14. *Major Policy Speeches by President Ngo Dinh Diem*, p. 43.

[4] Phuc Thien, *op. cit.*, pp. 9, 10.

[5] *Vietnam Press*, No. 299 (October 26, 1959, noon), p. VIII.

[6] Pham Quynh, *Essais Franco-Annamites* (1929-1932), (Hue: Editions Bui Huy Tin, 1937).

[7] "Summary of President Diem's Two Years in Power," *News Roundup* [USOM Vietnamese press translations daily bulletin], No. 002 (January, 1957), p. 9.

[8] *Vietnam Presse*, No. 2149 (January 3, 1957, *soir*), p. III (tr.)

[9] *Ibid.*, No. 2153, (January 7, 1957, *midi*), p. II.

[10] *Vietnam Press, Weekly English Series*, No. 81, (April 29, 1959), pp. 25-27. Hereafter this publication will be cited as VNP, WES. The daily series cited will be distinguishable as *Vietnam Press* (English language edition), if followed by one of the following release time designations: morning, noon, evening, or unique edition; and *Vietnam Presse* (French langauge edition), if followed by *matin, midi, soir, or édition unique.*

[11] *Times of Vietnam*, December 27, 1958, p. 1.

[12] *News Roundup*, exact date unknown.

[13] VNP, WES, No. 14, (January 4, 1958), p. 3.

[14] *Times of Vietnam*, June 28, 1958, p. 12; July 5, 1958, p. 5. Hereafter cited as *Times of VN*.

[15] "Confucianism and Personalism," *Times of VN*, September 29, 1956, p. I.

[16] *Bai Tuyen-Cao Cua Ban Quan-Tri Lam-Thoi, Hoi Khong-Hoc Vietnam [Manifesto of the Provisional Directing Committee of the Confucian Study Association]* (Saigon: date not indicated); published also in *Minh Tan* [newspaper] (Saigon), No. I (April 20, 1957), pp. I, 4. (tr.).

[17] VNP, WES. No. 24 (March 16, 1958), p. 14.

[18] VNP, No. 2207 (March 3, 1957, *édition unique*), p. IX (tr.).

[19] Many of Maritain's and Mounier's works are relevant to the following discussion and cannot be cited in detail. A complete bibliography of Mounier's extensive writings is included in the December, 1950 memorial issue of *Esprit* dedicated to him. Among the principal books which should at least be mentioned are: Maritain's *L'Humanisme Intégrale, Primauté du Spirituel, The Person and the Common Good, The Rights of Man and Natural Law,* and *Redeeming the Time*; and Mounier's *Révolution personnaliste et communautaire, Manifeste au service du personnalisme, Introduction aux existentialismes, Qu'est-ce que le personnalisme?* and *Le Personnalisme.*

[20] Personalism in this sense is not related to *personalismo*, which denotes "democratic caesarism" in Venezuela and refers to a doctrine of highly personalized political party leadership at the various organizational levels in Puerto Rico. On the Christian Democratic movement and its emphases on personalism, especially in France and Italy and also in Holland (where the new post-liberation Labor Party advocated "personalistic socialism"), Belgium, Western Germany and Austria, see Mario Einaudi and François Goguel, *Christian Democracy in Italy and France* (Notre Dame: University of Notre Dame Press, 1952). Maritain says 'personalism is not one school or a doctrine, but a "phenomenon of reaction against two opposite errors"—the individualism of the nineteenth century and "totalitarianism or the exclusively communal conception of society which took place by way of reaction. There are at least a dozen personalist doctrines, which, at times, have nothing more in common than the term 'person' . . . Some tend toward dictatorship, while others incline toward anarchy. A principal concern of Thomistic personalism is to avoid both excesses." (*The Person and the Common Good* [New York: Scribner's, 1947], pp. 2-3.)

[21] John T. Marcus, "Social Catholicism in Postwar France," *South Atlantic Quarterly*, Summer, 1957, p. 304.

[22] Emmanuel Mounier, *Le Personnalisme* (Paris: Presses Universitaires de France, 1955), p. 128.

[23] Einaudi and Goguel, *op cit.*, pp. 119-120.

[24] Ngo Dinh Nhu, "Why We Must Defend the Existing Regime," a talk delivered to Information Department officials in Saigon on November 15, 1957.

[25] Message to opening session of the National Assembly, October 6, 1958 quoted in *News from Vietnam* (Washington: Embassy of Vietnam), November 10, 1958, p. 6.

[26] Gordon Wright, "Catholics and Peasantry in France," *Political Science Quarterly*, December, 1953, pp. 526-551. Collective cultivation of part of a village's acreage is a traditional practice particularly in North and Central Vietnam, incidentally, and it is being followed in some of the new resettlement communities in the highlands.

[27] VNP, WES, No. 66 (January 18, 1959), p. 11; *Times of VN*, February 28, 1959, p. 3.

[28] Gordon Wright, *op. cit.*, pp. 536-540.

[29] J. B. Coates, *The Crisis of the Human Person* (London: Longmans, Green, 1949), Chapter 1.

[30] *Times of VN Magazine*, July 11, 1959, pp. 3-4.

[31] Lunar New Year Message for 1960, VNP, WES, January 31, 1960, p. 2.

[32] VNP, No. 2158 (January 12, 1957, *midi*), pp. IV-VI (tr.).

[33] "Social Principles of the Asian Traditional Philosophies," made to the Euro-Asian Trade Union Seminar in January, 1959. *Times of VN*, January 31, 1959, pp. 7, 9. This is discussed further below.

[34] *Ibid.*; also, Ngo Dinh Diem's speech at Seoul University, September 21, 1957.

[35] Dean Bao gives as the chief "Western" values the stress on reason and law, technology (stemming from theoretical science along with mass production for mass consumption) and the "Christian Miracle" of the assimilation of Greek and Roman secular values in a transcendental system emphasizing a Divinity. The chief "Eastern" values, he suggests, are the following: love of life, as manifested in the Easterner's fondness for large families and in the Confucian embodiment of law and justice in a person; nature, and man's pantheistic way of identifying with nature instead of "distinguishing [between] Man, God and Nature"; respect for the past, tradition and old age; and the cult of the family. He then suggests that Easterners and Westerners are fundamentally similar in the identical capacity for love and sacrifice, identical revolt against injustice, identical gesture of worship before beauty and ". . . the equal distribution of Reason among all men. . . . What is fundamental is the existence of the same moral conscience in every climate." Such values, therefore, are not Eastern or Western but essentially "Human Values and belong to the Commonwealth of Humanity . . ." United Nations Day address, 1957, published in *Dai Hoc Van Khoa [Annales de la Faculté des Lettres de Saigon]*, 1957-1958 (Saigon: University of Saigon, Faculty of Letters, 1958).

An extensive list of projects designed to advance the investigation of ways to harmonize Western and Eastern values, many of them undertaken with UNESCO aid, is given in *La République du Vietnam et Le Projet Majeur Orient-Occident* by Nguyen Khac Kham, Secretary General of the National Commission for UNESCO, published by the Department of Education, 1959.

[36] VNP, WES, No. 6 (November 9, 1957), pp. 2-5.

[37] *Khai-Niem Ve Chu-Nghia Nhan Vi [A General Conception of Personalism]*, [Saigon, 1960?]

[38] F. C. Copleston, *Aquinas (Baltimore: Penguin Books, 1955), p. 239.*

[39] A few months later this group published a book by Pham Dinh Kiem, *Seeking to Understand the Social Problem [Tim Hieu Van-De Xa-Hoi]*, which will be discussed below along with the rest of these private formulations.

[40] This work also will be included in the summary discussion of these monographs below.

[41] These works available in book form include the following: Manh Dat, *The Concept of Vietnamese Personalism [Quan-Niem Nhan-Vi Viet-Nam]*, (Saigon: Loai Sach Hoc Tap, 1957). Truc Lam Linh, *Personalist Light: A Popular Conversation in Verse [Anh Sang Nhan-Vi; Tho Pho-Thong Doi-Thoai]* (Saigon: Thanh-Long, 1956). Tran Huu Thanh, *The Personalist Revolution [Cuoc Cach-Mang Nhan-Vi]* (Saigon: [1955]). Huy Thinh, *Notions of the Personalist Doctrine [Khai-Niem Hoc-Thuyet Nhan-Vi]*, [1956]. Le Thanh Tri, *Doctrine of a Personalist, Spiritual Society [Hoc-Thuyet Xa-Hoi Nhan-Vi Duy-Linh]* (Saigon: Tu Sach Triet Hoc, 1957). Bui Tuan, *Personalism, the Basis for Reconstruction [Xay Dung Tren Nhan-Vi]* (Hue: Nhan Thuc, 1956). Huy Tuan and Hoai Thinh, *Concrete Aspects of President Ngo's Personalism [The-Hien Nhan-Vi Cua Ngo Tong-Thong]* (Saigon: Nghien Cuu, 1956). Nguyen Dinh Viet, *The Personalist View of Leadership [Quan-Niem Nhan-Vi Ve Lanh-Dao]* (Saigon: Gio Len, 1956).

[42] Huy Thinh, *op. cit.*, pp. 12-14.

[43] *Dai-Hoi Van-Hoa Viet-Nam*, 1957, p. 50.

[44] *Ibid.*, pp. 47-48.

[45] *Ibid.*, p. 89.

[46] Tran Huu Thanh, *op. cit.*, p. 80.

[47] *Ibid.*, p. 82.

[48] Manh Dat, *op. cit.*, p. 67.

[49] Nguyen Dinh Viet, *op. cit.*, pp. 43-44.

[50] Tran Huu Thanh, *op. cit.*, pp. 42-43; Manh Dat, *op. cit.*, pp. 45-47.

[51] Tran Huu Thanh, *op. cit.*, pp. 45-46, 79.

[52] *Ibid.*, pp. 44-45.

[53] *Ibid.*, pp. 88-89.

[54] Huy Tuan and Hoai Thinh, *op. cit.*, p. 54.

[55] Lunar New Year [Tet] Message, 1959, VNP, WES, No. 71 (February 15, 1959), pp. 2-3.

[56] "Why We Must Defend the Existing Regime," *op. cit.* Just what measures the government may adopt to get the people to make available such investment funds remains to be seen. Article 21 of the Constitution provides, incidentally, that "The State shall facilitate the use of savings in acquiring dwellings, agricultural land and shares in business corporations."

[57] *Times of VN Magazine*, July 23, 1960, pp. 3, 21; August 6, p. 21; September 10, pp. 3, 20.

[58] VNP, WES, No. 31 (May 4, 1958), pp. 16-18.

[59] See, *supra*, that part of the text referred to by Note 30.

[60] *Times of VN*, March 28, 1959, p. 3.

[61] *Times of VN*, September 20, 1958, p, 3; VNP, WES, No. 50, September 14, 1958, p. 15.

[62] *Times of VN Magazine*, July 23, 1960, pp. 3, 21.

[63] "P. J. H.," "Progress in the Republic of Viet-Nam," *Times of VN*, March 28, 1959, p. 6. This article originally was published in *The World Today*, February 1959, pp. 68-78, and a somewhat abridged two-part version of it was run in the *Times of VN* of this date and of April 4, 1959.

[64] *Times of VN*, May 14, 1960, p. 10.

[65] *Ibid.*, February 23, 1957, p. 3.

[66] VNP, No. 2162 (January 16, 1957, *soir*), p. VIII; and No. 2208 (March 4, 1957, *matin*), p. X.

[67] *Times of VN*, June 7, 1958, p. 4.

[68] *Ibid.*, January 28, 1956, p. I.

[69] VNP, WES, No. 29 (April 20, 1958), pp. 18, 19.

[70] "Adultery by the wife, even if duly proven, is not in itself a cause of disavowal" by the husband but his suit will be considered by the court if his wife bears the child of another man (*Family Code*, Article 86.).

[71] *Family Code*, Chapter III, Sections I and II.

[72] *Times of VN*, December 21, 1957, p. 8.

[73] *Ibid.*, June 28, 1958, p. 7. President Ngo's recommendations for minor rephrasing of parts of four articles and the addition of one new article (enabling a wife or husband in certain situations to apply to a court for confiscation of the spouse's income) were passed by the Assembly without opposition before promulgation—see *ibid.*, December 20, 1958, p. 3, and January 10, 1959, pp. 4, 12.

[74] *Ibid.*, January 31, 1959, p. 3.

[75] *Ibid.*, June 28, 1958.

[76] *Times of VN*, March 14, 1959, pp. 1, 4, 8. The North Vietnam National Assembly passed a new family law on December 29, 1959, based on the "four principles of free and independent marriage, monogamy, equality between husband and wife" and the guarantee of the rights of women and children. It gives both spouses the right to sue for divorce, prohibits child marriage, forced marriage and "beating or other ill treatment of the wife" and sets minimum ages for marriage at 18 for women and 20 for men. (Broadcast by Radio Hanoi in English Morse to Southeast Asia, December 29, 1959).

[77] VNP, WES, No. 34 (May 25, 1958), p. 19; *Times of VN*, November 29, 1958, pp. 5, 12.

[78] VNP, WES, No. 36 (June 8, 1958), p. 19.

[79] VNP, WES, No. 122 (February 7, 1960), p. 7.

[80] VNP, WES, No. 36 (June 8, 1958), p. 4; *Times of VN*, June 14, 1958, pp. 3, 5; *ibid.*, July 26, 1958, p. 2.

[81] VNP, WES, No. 38 (June 22, 1958), p. 22.

[82] VNP, WES, No. 30 (April 27, 1958), p. 35.

[83] VNP, WES, No. 53 (October 5, 1958).

[84] *Times of VN*, May 10, 1958, p. 1.

[85] *Ibid.*, September 20, 1958, p. 6.

[86] VNP, WES, No. 30 (April 27, 1958), p. 35.

[87] Address at Seoul University, September 21, 1957.

[88] VNP, No. 422 (February 27, 1957, evening), pp. a-e.

[89] Information on these centers is scarce. The *Times of VN* of February 23, 1957 carried without comment an American correspondent's report that there probably were between 7,000 and 8,000 such prisoners at that time See also Wesley R. Fishel, "Vietnam's War of Attrition," *The New Leader*, December 7, 1959, p. 20.

[90] VNP, No. 2158 (January 12, 1957, *midi*), p. VII (tr.).

[91] Joseph Buttinger, *The Smaller Dragon* (New York: Praeger, 1958), pp. 160-161.

[92] "Influence des valeurs traditionnelles et des structures sociales sur les niveaux de vie," manu-

script of an address delivered to the seminar on "Social Research and Problems of Rural Life in Southeast Asia" in Saigon in March, 1960.

[93] C. K. Yang, "The Functional Relationship between Confucian Thought and Chinese Religion," in John K. Fairbank, ed., *Chinese Thought and Institutions* (Chicago: Univ. of Chicago Press, 1957), pp. 269-290.

[94] *The Disposition of Buddhist Temples in Vietnam: The Composition of the Buddhist Pantheon*, Special Edition published by the magazine *Horizons* (Saigon: 1956).

[95] Christianity was introduced into Vietnam by Portuguese missionaries in the sixteenth century. Latest available figures indicate that Catholics in Free Vietnam total about 1,015,914, constituting about 7.3 per cent of a total population estimated at 13,882,575. There are also several thousand Protestants. These figures on Catholics are issued by Vietnamese Catholic authorities as reported in VNP, WES, December 13, 1960, pp. 12-13. The population figure, based on both counts and estimates, is from Lloyd W. Woodruff, assisted by Nguyen Ngoc Yen, *Local Administration in Viet-Nam; The Number of Local Units*, Michigan State University Advisory Group, National Institute of Administration, Republic of Viet-Nam, Saigon, Report No. 1, Local Administration Series, Nov. 1, 1960, p. 5.

[96] VNP, WES, December 27, 1959, p. 2.

[97] J. A. C. Grant, "The Vietnam Constitution of 1956," *American Political Science Review*, June 1958, p. 444.

[98] Gordon Wright, *op. cit.*, p. 550.

[99] H. G. Fairbanks, "What is Personalism?" *Times of VN Magazine*, May 14, 1960, p. 11.

[100] *Times of VN*, November 21, 1959, p. 14. This passage is from an article published originally in *Asian Culture* (Saigon), I, No. 4.

[101] *Ibid.*, January 3, 1959, pp. 7, 9, 12. This article was published originally in *Asian Culture*, I, No. 1.

[102] William T. de Bary, ed., *Sources of the Indian Tradition* (New York: Columbia University Press, 1958), p. 572. For rejecting the divinity of Christ, Rammohun became embroiled in controversy with Protestant missionaries in Calcutta but his movement, the *Brahmo Samaj*, or Society of God, lived on and exists as a minor element in contemporary Indian religious philosophy.

[103] Information obtained in correspondence from Saigon.

[104] For a discussion of the Constitution's "Bill of Rights" and other provisions defining the status of the citizen and a comparison of them with actual practice including harrassment of editors, administrative imprisonment, etc., see J. A. C. Grant, *op. cit.*, pp. 437-462. For additional background on the wider problem, see also William Henderson, "South Viet Nam Finds Itself," *Foreign Affairs*, January, 1957, pp. 283-294; Ellen J. Hammer, "Progress Report on Southern Viet Nam," *Pacific Affairs*, September, 1957, pp. 221-235; John T. Dorsey, Jr., "South Viet Nam in Perspective," *Far Eastern Survey*, December, 1958; various articles by Wesley R. Fishel and particularly his chapter in this book.

[105] The present writer believes that additional political research in Vietnam, which he plans to conduct soon, will be requisite to his forming a judgment on this question any more complete than the tentative and fragmentary conclusions presented in this paper.

[106] Daniel Bell, *The End of Ideology* (Glencoe, Ill.: Free Press, 1960), p. 373.

[107] VNP, WES, No. 56 (October 26, 1958), p. 1.

CHAPTER 4

Vietnam's Concept of Development

*by Vu Van Thai**

SINCE THE SUBJECT of this meeting is the social progress of Vietnam, the presence of its Director of the Budget, an economist, may appear somewhat odd. While I desired the pleasure of being with friends of my country, many of whom are in addition personal friends, I feel compelled to justify my functional presence here. If my President has chosen me to come here, it is because our concept of development is a total concept, and it is not possible to separate our concept of economic growth from our concept of social and political development.

To us balanced growth does not mean merely economic development but also balance between economic, social and political development. There has been a general tendency to consider the process of growth of under-developed countries as a process aiming at an increase in the rate of capital formation. In our view the development must aim at change in social and economic structure tending to create a society where each people will have the necessary conditions to fulfill its material, cultural and spiritual needs. In order to achieve this goal, the process of development must aim at changing the social structure and creating the political sub-structure, as well as tending to develop the productive capacity of the country.

There has been a general tendency to conceive economic development as a maximum sacrifice of the present in order to build the future. In our concept we hold that the process of growth can take place by enlarging the demand as well as the supply, and that it is not only important to save but to use the saving in such a way as to necessitate a minimum sacrifice on the part of the population. It is for this reason that, contrary to the general tendency in many newly independent Asian countries, we do not give particular priority to industrialization.

*Vu Van Thai was the Director-General of Budget and Foreign Aid, Government of the Republic of Vietnam until August, 1961.

69

Instead we are encouraging agricultural development complemented by progressive industrialization. To our mind this is the best way to build the social and economic sub-structure on which to base our future industrial development, and the way that leads to the minimum of sacrifice for the best results.

Since there is much available land in our country, the development of agricultural production requires less capital than that of industrial production. If productivity is an important factor in raising the standard of living, then it is relatively less costly for us to catch up with the agricultural productivity level of developed countries than with their industrial productivity. And since our population lacks a fully balanced diet, an improvement in agricultural development has human as well as economic value.

In fact, economic growth can be realized only if the population takes an active part in it. Improvement in the health and physical energy of the people is a prerequisite for their active participation. Another advantage resulting from agricultural development should be an increased propensity to save, this being one of the main conditions for a quick and over-all economic growth. So long as the population remains underfed, it cannot be expected to set aside part of its income for productive saving.

It is only by satisfying primary needs that we can facilitate the future formation of domestic capital capable of replacing foreign financial aid. An increased income for the rural population will result in the greater purchasing power required to foster industrial production. It must be understood, however, that all the foregoing considerations do not negate the usefulness of a complementary industrialization. This is necessary if we are to have a well-balanced growth.

At the present time, it is evident that light industry, producing consumer goods, is urgently needed to reduce imports and balance our foreign trade. Later on, with an increased rural income, the demand for manufactured goods will be increased at the same time that technical improvements in agriculture liberate a growing volume of labor. Industry will provide the liaison between the labor supply and the demand for manufactured goods. In this way there will be no industrialization forced on the country at the price of heavy sacrifice. But, instead, a progressive industrialization will take place, induced by general economic growth.

Complementary agricultural industry is also useful because it will create a market for products such as sugar cane, cotton and tea. Diversification in agricultural production will thereby be made possible.

Economic progress will thus affect every sector of the economy, and contribute to the well-being of the whole population. This is our choice instead of a process that will result in the setting up of an industrially organized sector in juxtaposition to an agricultural sector living at a subsistence level and involving most of the population.

Another difficult problem that must be faced is our inability to follow the process of growth of the now-developed countries in which the accumulation and acceleration of capital formation has been realized mainly through concentration of capital and income in a few hands. The adoption of a development plan based mainly on agriculture together with a complementary industrialization will allow us to accelerate capital formation without passing through a phase in which concentration of capital is in the hands of the few. By such a device as agrarian reform, there is a mobilization of capital in agriculture for the building of industry. And we can thus achieve social capitalism without passing through a stage of concentrated capitalism.

Having thus chosen our process of growth, we must ask ourselves whether to have production intended for a foreign or domestic market. The point is this: Must we return to the pre-war specialization of producing primary products intended for export? It is clear that the past specialization in production for export was partially responsible for the extreme poverty of the population. Some figures will be sufficient to point out the paradoxical pre-war situation. While its population was one of the most underfed, Vietnam exported one-third of its rice and about five-sixths of its corn, these being the principal and almost sole food crops.

While the production of cotton could have been attempted on a large scale with a great deal of labor employed on the production of cotton cloth, especially since imported fabrics of cotton represented and still represent one of our largest imports, all labor driven from agriculture was directed either to the rubber plantations whose whole production was exported, or to the coal mines. One third of the coal produced was sufficient to cover domestic needs. Thus the specialization in production for export resulted in the production of food stuffs for foreign markets while there was an unsatisfied domestic demand, as well as in the production of industrial raw materials for which there was no demand at home. This production potential could have alleviated the misery of the population if it had been utilized for increasing production for domestic consumption. As long as the domestic demand consists mainly of food, clothing, and housing, which will be true for many years to come, and as long as this need can be met by domestic production, it is this potential which should be developed first.

In short, economic development should be undertaken in accordance with the balanced-growth principle, which means that the activities to be favored must first be those for which there is a potential domestic market. Of course, it will be necessary to proceed with the development of some exports in profitable economic sectors to match the necessary import of capital goods and the need of other foreign payments.

This approach allows us to avoid somewhat the dilemma of allocation of resources between social and economic development. Because we have chosen the path of minimum sacrifice for the quickest and best results in increased production, we are able to allocate relatively more resources to social improvement without imposing too great a burden on the population. On the other hand, we plan to develop a social program that will tend to reinforce our economic development and create a social structure adapted to our economic program. This is why education is given a particular priority, and why we have made a greater effort to develop primary and basic education than higher education. This is in accordance with our view that development must involve the whole population and not just the elite.

Our determination to associate the creation of a new social structure with increased production is not limited only to our concept of economic development, but is also reflected in the choice and development of specific projects. Let me, for instance, cite the case of the land development project in the highlands. This development does not stem only from our *desire* to increase our production and diversify our agricultural capacity—it has been undertaken for other considerations. The first is the need for geographical balance in our development; we want to involve the whole country in the development process. The second is the desirability of changing the traditions of Vietnam's people from those of a people of the plains into those of a people of both plains and highlands. These projects have been implemented so as to modify the structure of village life by resettling people in larger villages than was traditionally common. This allows the supply of better social services such as schools, hospitals, maternity clinics, and the like, and encourages the development of community projects which in turn increase social facilities in the villages.

Besides the land projects in the highlands, we have undertaken similar ones elsewhere in places as widespread as possible. In such places we have been able to change the attitude of the people and the structure of rural life, changing the villages into big rural centers with more community life and some common use of the facilities of production such as tractors. The example of these new centers will gradually extend to neighboring areas, and change progressively the whole structure of rural life.

At the same time, an effort is being made to deconcentrate the towns and thus avoid proletarization of city workers.

Our emphasis on light industry fits into this program of deconcentration and humanization of life in the city and will ultimately make possible a liaison by which handicrafts and industry can become an association more than a competition.

As we see it, development has to be regarded as a three-dimensional process measured in terms of economic, social, and political improvement, for in our present under-development and low living standards, the achievement of human dignity and political freedom is primarily a matter of improving the economic condition of the people.

This, more than any form of political organization, represents the most effective way towards the establishment of a true democratic structure. Viewed in such a light, a process of development which does not put an excessive burden on people already on a subsistence level is our concept of democratic growth.

CHAPTER 5

Problems of Education In Vietnam

by Edgar N. Pike*

ORIGINS OF VIETNAMESE EDUCATION

Public and private education in Vietnam today represents a striking evolution from the Mandarin elite system inherited from the Chinese, through a gradual modernization and a selective French-administered system, to the present-day dedication to universal education.

Although the early education system was only codified in 622 A. D., it probably dates back to the beginning of the Christian era. Earliest records indicate the solemnity and prestige attributed to the acquisition of learning. Wealth, power, and military prowess were considered lesser virtues than knowledge, and young girls in quest of marriage preferred the straw mat of the frail and shivering scholar to the satin lounges of the landlords and merchants.

Despite the considerable influence of India, Vietnam's educational system, like that of Korea and Japan, was first built upon the Chinese cultural pattern, and its language written in Chinese ideographs. Essentially it was a Confucian system with later Buddhist influences.

At the age of six, boys began their schooling by bringing the schoolmaster a cock to be sacrificed in a Confucian commemoration of the dawning of intelligence. In private or family schools or from tutors, students learned to commit classic texts to memory and reproduce them with delicate brush strokes. Those who succeeded in their Tieu-hoc (Little Studies) were accepted at 15 as candidates for an examination that required three years of study as preparation, and from the group that succeeded in passing were sifted the students of the Dai-hoc (Greater Studies) in the Four Canonical Books and the Five Sacred Books.

---

*Edgar N. Pike is with the Asia Foundation, San Francisco, and directed its activities in Vietnam, 1955-1959. He is currently its representative in the Republic of China.

75

Graduation, or the passing of the difficult examinations, was a glorious achievement. Feted by the Emperor, the students would receive according to their ratings a palanquin, a horse, or other gift, and return in triumph to their native villages.

Quite often, the student would not complete the various stages of learning—"flowering talent," "elevated man" and, in the royal examinations, the highest degree of "teacher"—until his fortieth year. He would then be tapped for the highest of government posts and he and his family could be forever assured of honors and respect.

Aside from the upper classes, some children in family or private schools (there were few primary schools) financed by village or family groups, would learn the minimum Chinese characters that would permit them to read and write pagoda notices and bills of sale, and decipher the ancestral names on the family altar. A few state schools did exist at the primary and secondary levels for study prerequisite to the Quoc Tu Giam (Imperial College).

In the last great examinations in Hanoi in 1876 and 1879, six thousand candidates were examined for civil service positions before the Mandarin scholars. Thereafter, with a few exceptions, the French schools began to replace the Mandarin system. The last academic examinations based on Vietnamese traditional programs were held in 1918.

The aim of Mandarin education was to form "loyal and virtuous men." The study of literature and moral principles was designed to develop loyalty to the sovereign, respect for parents, faithfulness to friends, and kindness to others. The purpose of education was to train men for government. Manual labor was considered degrading and, as a result, technical education was totally neglected.

Under the French, education became more specific in its intent to train selected adjuncts to the colonial administration, to produce a limited number of clerical subordinates and interpreters. Through the efforts of dedicated educators it had, however, begun to evolve into a potentially excellent and well-balanced system. Its most unfortunate legacy was its exaggerated emphasis on the diploma, whose symbolic and status value became more important to the students than the education it was intended to symbolize. The effect of this emphasis has lingered in the attitude of the average Vietnamese toward education; it will be discussed in a later section of this paper. No attempt will be made here to detail the history of Vietnamese education during the colonial period; it was a history of slow progress in a system transplanted from France, accompanied by the increasing Westernization of the cities. Since the countryside was slower to change, the result was an increasing gap in understanding between the educated and the uneducated, between the civil servant and intellectual and the tiller of the land.

Education is primarily a reflection of the values and needs of the society it serves. Under the French most executive technicians and administrators were supplied by the *metropole*, while the Vietnamese only gradually climbed upward in subordinate roles or in areas that had previously been reserved for the colonial power. Education was based on the "two-track" system—that is, it had one plan for potential leaders, who would go on to higher education, and another leading to vocational training. In practice the system produced an over-abundance of "intellectuals" and but few trained specialists. At Independence, then, there was an enormous gap between the number of trained personnel needed to take over the immense quantity of government and private administrative positions and the number available. This gap is generally the most significant obstacle to progress in underdeveloped countries, and Vietnam is no exception. Expansion of the educational system had become a frantic necessity.

PROBLEMS OF EDUCATIONAL CHANGE AND EXPANSION

The need for skills, the importance of agricultural and technical education, are obvious in Southeast Asia. But equally vital is the need for quality, for the kind of creative men and women who can make a system work. Students can easily learn rules and regulations, memorize decrees and laws, and become familiar with other aspects of complex twentieth-century society. But for any system to work, there must be people with imagination, initiative, and the ability to see through the complexities to the purposes of the society. If we have learned anything in the great re-examination of education now taking place in America, it is that intelligent children will rise to meet higher standards and the most complex challenges and, conversely, that if standards are reduced to the lowest common denominator, students' interest and abilities will be correspondingly reduced. Vietnam is not exempt from the latter hazard, which is inherent in too-hasty an attempt at mass education, and its leaders know it. The need for technical training must be balanced against the need for enlightened and flexible leadership. In all societies, there is always powerful resistance to changes in education, and the seed must be planted solidly before reforms can take root.

Tran Huu The, Minister of Education, defined the principles of Vietnamese education in a major policy speech given in March of 1959.

The similarity of some of Vietnam's educational aims to our own is striking, in its recognition that mass education can submerge what the Rockefeller Report calls "the pursuit of excellence." Mr. The says emphatically: "A diploma is merely an attestation of a technical character. It is not an end, but a beginning. Our children must realize that they study to become men, and not simply to obtain a diploma."

EDUCATIONAL ROADBLOCK:
THE DIPLOMA AS STATUS SYMBOL

One of the most serious problems confronting educators in Vietnam is the high status value of the diploma. The diploma stands, in the Vietnamese cultural attitude, for the attainment of a stable, privileged position in society. The student is thus motivated toward gaining a degree, toward the symbol and not toward the thing for which it stands. Thus the passing of examinations has become so important that secondary school students have been known to commit suicide when they failed—and a diploma can be the mark of a closed rather than an open mind, the achievement of a fixed position in society rather than the beginning of a process of self-improvement.

In general the Vietnamese student (male or female, for women are increasingly important in the nation) is serious about his studies, and knows that the acquisition of a diploma will affect his status and role in society for his whole life. He is respectful to his teachers and reluctant to ask questions. He will polish up his lecture notes at the library, but will do little outside reading except under direct pressure from the teacher, and has little access to materials on current events. Often his secondary school subjects are more advanced than those offered in the average American school. He is quick to learn languages and assiduous in his work, but has little curiosity about the whys and hows of the facts he accumulates. His first preference for a career tends to be medicine or law, and his ambitions are usually directed toward a permanent civil service job. The pressures of tradition and status set him apart from the uneducated, but when he is presented with opportunities for social service (such as work camps) he can display remarkable idealism and will volunteer his services readily. In general he is inclined to be concerned with security rather than experiment or adventure. Thus there is little of the fiery political activity normally found on Asian campuses. The Vietnamese student often abjures politics completely, in his cautious concern for his family and his personal advancement. Certain convictions he does develop slowly

TABLE 7
DOMICILE OF FAMILY UNITS OF INTERVIEWEES WHO ARE MARRIED, DIVORCED OR WIDOWED

Domicile	Number	Percent
Living with nuclear family	69	43.9
Living with extended family	69	43.9
Living with friends	9	5.7
Living without family and boarding	10	6.4
Total	157	99.9

TABLE 8
COMPARISON OF ADULT POPULATION OF SAIGON WITH WORK FORCE IN SAMPLE, BY LITERACY LEVEL IN VIETNAMESE

	Sample	Census [1]
Level of Literacy	Percent	Percent
Illiterate	23.8	28.3
Reading and writing	76.2	71.7
Total	100.0	100.0

[1] Data for the adult population, ages 15-60, are compiled from *Enquête Demographique à Saigon, Juin-Juillet 1958* (Resultats Provisoires), Institut National de la Statistique.

TABLE 9
MONTHLY INCOME OF EMPLOYEES IN SAMPLE WORK FORCE BY TYPE OF JOB SKILL

Monthly Income ($VN)	Skilled #	Skilled %	Semi-Skilled #	Semi-Skilled %	Unskilled #	Unskilled %	Clerical #	Clerical %	Total #	Total %
999 or less	—	—	6	14.3	55	47.8	—	—	61	26.9
1000-1499	13	20.3	17	40.5	48	41.7	—	—	78	34.4
1500-1999	10	15.6	9	21.4	6	5.2	1	16.7	26	11.4
2000-2499	14	21.9	7	16.6	4	3.5	2	33.3	27	11.9
2500-2999	11	17.2	1	2.4	1	0.9	—	—	13	5.7
3000-3499	4	6.3	1	2.4	—	—	—	—	5	2.2
3500-3999	5	7.8	—	—	—	—	2	33.3	7	3.1
4000 and over	7	10.9	1	2.4	1	0.9	1	16.7	10	4.4
Total	64	100.0	42	100.0	115	100.0	6	100.0	227	100.0

TABLE 10
MONTHLY INCOME OF EMPLOYEES IN SAMPLE WORK FORCE, BY SEX OF INTERVIEWEE

Monthly Income ($VN)	Male Number	Male Percent	Female Number	Female Percent	Total Number	Total Percent
999 or less	9	5.8	52	73.3	61	26.9
1000-1499	64	41.0	14	19.7	78	34.4
1500-1999	24	15.4	2	2.8	26	11.4
2000-2499	26	16.7	1	1.4	27	11.9
2500-2999	13	8.3	—	—	13	5.7
3000-3499	5	3.2	—	—	5	2.2
3500-3999	6	3.8	1	1.4	7	3.1
4000 and over	9	5.8	1	1.4	10	4.4
Total	156	100.0	71	100.0	227	100.0

TABLE 11
LENGTH OF TIME IN PRESENT PLACE OF EMPLOYMENT, BY AGE OF EMPLOYEE

Length of Employment	Age of Employee																			Total	
	Under 20		20-24		25-29		30-34		35-39		40-44		45-49		50-54		55 and over				
	#	%	#	%	#	%	#	%	#	%	#	%	#	%	#	%	#	%	#	%		
Less than one year	8	22.2	3	5.5	1	3.7	2	8.0	2	9.4	1	5.9	—	—	—	—	—	—	17	7.5		
1-2 years	23	63.9	19	35.2	10	37.1	7	28.0	1	4.8	4	23.5	5	23.8	1	7.7	1	7.7	71	31.3		
3-4 years	5	13.9	15	27.8	8	29.6	5	20.0	1	4.8	2	11.8	3	14.4	—	—	1	7.7	40	17.6		
5-6 years	—	—	9	16.7	2	7.4	1	4.0	6	28.6	3	17.6	—	—	3	23.1	—	—	24	10.6		
7-8 years	—	—	7	13.0	2	7.4	4	16.0	4	19.0	3	17.6	4	19.0	2	15.4	2	15.4	28	12.3		
9-10 years	—	—	—	—	4	14.8	4	16.0	1	4.8	2	11.8	4	19.0	1	7.7	1	7.7	17	7.5		
11 years or more	—	—	1	1.8	—	—	2	8.0	6	28.6	2	11.8	5	23.8	6	46.1	8	61.5	30	13.2		
Total	36	100.0	54	100.0	27	100.0	25	100.0	21	100.0	17	100.0	21	100.0	13	100.0	13	100.0	227	100.0		

TABLE 12

PREVIOUS EMPLOYMENT OF EMPLOYEES IN SAMPLE WORK FORCE,
BY SEX OF INTERVIEWEE

Job Status	Male		Female		Total	
	#	%	#	%	#	%
Previously employed	92	59.0	15	21.1	107	47.1
Not previously employed	64	41.0	56	78.9	120	52.9
Total	156	100.0	71	100.0	227	100.0

TABLE 13

COMPARISON OF NATIVE BORN ADULT POPULATION OF SAIGON
WITH WORK FORCE IN SAMPLE, BY PLACE OF BIRTH

Place of Birth	Census [1]	Sample
	Percent	Percent
South Viet Nam	35.2	21.0
Saigon	31.2	69.4
North Viet Nam	25.8	7.2
Central Viet Nam and the Plateau Region (PMS)	7.8	2.4
Total	100.0	100.0

[1] Data from the adult population, ages 15-60, are compiled from *Enquête Demographique à Saigon, Juin-Juillet 1958* (Resultats Provisoires), Institut National de la Statistique.

TABLE 14

EDUCATIONAL BACKGROUND OF EMPLOYEES IN THE SAMPLE

WORK FORCE, BY PLACE OF BIRTH

Educational Background	Saigon and Suburbs		South Viet Nam		Central Viet Nam		North Viet Nam		Foreign Born		Total	
	Number	Percent	Number	Percent	Number	Percent	Number	Percent	Number	Percent	Number	Percent
Illiterate	29	20.0	5	11.4	1	20.0	4	26.7	15	83.3	54	23.8
Some reading and writing	67	46.2	15	34.1	2	40.0	4	26.7	3	16.7	91	40.1
Elementary school	41	28.3	15	34.1	2	40.0	2	13.3	—	—	60	26.4
Secondary school or beyond	8	5.5	9	20.4	—	—	5	33.3	—	—	22	9.7
Total	145	100.0	44	100.0	5	100.0	15	100.0	18	100.0	227	100.0

TABLE 15

JOB SKILLS IN THE SAMPLE WORK FORCE, BY PLACE OF BIRTH

Job Skill	Saigon and Suburbs		South Viet Nam		Central Viet Nam		North Viet Nam		Foreign Born		Total	
	Number	Percent	Number	Percent	Number	Percent	Number	Percent	Number	Percent	Number	Percent
Skilled	40	27.6	15	34.1	3	60.0	5	33.3	1	5.6	64	28.2
Semi-skilled	25	17.2	6	13.6	1	20.0	2	13.3	8	44.4	42	18.5
Unskilled	77	53.1	21	47.7	1	20.0	7	46.7	9	50.0	115	50.7
Clerical	3	2.1	2	4.6	—	—	1	6.7	—	—	6	2.6
Total	145	100.0	44	100.0	5	100.0	15	100.0	18	100.0	227	100.0

TABLE 16

PREFERENCE FOR PRESENT SITUATION OF EMPLOYEES IN SAMPLE

WORK FORCE, BY LENGTH OF TIME IN SAIGON[1]

Preference	Length of Time								Total	
	2 years or less		3-4 years		5-6 years		More than 6 years			
	Number	Percent	Number	Percent	Number	Percent	Number	Percent	Number	Percent
Prefer working in Saigon	8	88.9	15	83.3	3	100.0	47	90.4	73	89.0
Prefer return to village	1	11.1	3	16.7	—	—	5	9.6	9	11.0
Total	9	100.0	18	100.0	3	100.0	52	100.0	82	100.0

[1] Replies are tabulated only for those who have migrated to Saigon.

TABLE 17
REASONS ADVANCED FOR STAYING IN SAIGON BY EMPLOYEES
IN SAMPLE WORK FORCE[1]

Reasons	Number	Percent
Easier to find jobs	33	40.2
No place to return	28	34.1
Prefer city life	4	4.9
Family obligations	4	4.9
Reluctant to change residence	4	4.9
Other	6	7.3
No opinion	3	3.7
Total	82	100.0

[1] Replies are tabulated only for those who have migrated to Saigon.

TABLE 18
TRADE UNION MEMBERSHIP OF EMPLOYEES IN SAMPLE WORK FORCE, BY JOB SKILL

Status	Skilled Number	Skilled Percent	Semi-skilled Number	Semi-skilled Percent	Unskilled Number	Unskilled Percent	Clerical Number	Clerical Percent	Total Number	Total Percent
Member	16	25.0	25	59.5	56	48.7	1	16.7	98	43.2
Non-member	48	75.0	17	40.5	59	51.3	5	83.3	129	56.8
Total	64	100.0	42	100.0	115	100.0	6	100.0	227	100.0

TABLE 19
TRADE UNION MEMBERSHIP OF EMPLOYEES IN SAMPLE WORK
FORCE, BY SEX OF INTERVIEWEE

Status	Male Number	Male Percent	Female Number	Female Percent	Total Number	Total Percent
Member	59	37.8	39	54.9	98	43.2
Non-member	97	62.2	32	45.1	129	56.8
Total	156	100.0	71	100.0	227	100.0

TABLE 20

TRADE UNION MEMBERSHIP OF EMPLOYEES IN SAMPLE WORK FORCE, BY CITIZENSHIP OF INTERVIEWEE

Status	Vietnamese		Naturalized Vietnamese		Foreign Citizen		Total	
	Number	Percent	Number	Percent	Number	Percent	Number	Percent
Member	77	39.9	11	64.7	10	58.8	98	43.2
Non-member	116	60.1	6	35.3	7	41.2	129	56.8
Total	193	100.0	17	100.0	17	100.0	227	100.0

TABLE 21

LABOR UNION MEMBERSHIP OF EMPLOYEES IN SAMPLE WORK FORCE,

BY PLANTS IN THE SAMPLE

Status	Plant A		Plant B		Plant C		Plant D		Total	
	Number	Percent	Number	Percent	Number	Percent	Number	Percent	Number	Percent
Member	10	11.9	3	8.6	36	73.5	49	83.1	98	43.2
Non-member	74	88.1	32	91.4	13	26.5	10	16.9	129	56.8
Total	84	100.0	35	100.0	49	100.0	59	100.0	227	100.0

TABLE 22

COMPARISON OF STATEMENTS ON JOB SATISFACTION BY EMPLOYEES
IN THE SAMPLE WORK FORCE, BY JOB SKILL[1]

Job Satisfaction	Skilled		Semi-skilled		Unskilled		Clerical		Total	
	Number	Percent	Number	Percent	Number	Percent	Number	Percent	Number	Percent
Present job most satisfactory	20	46.5	16	59.2	17	48.6	1	50.0	54	50.5
No job has been satisfactory	19	44.2	9	33.4	11	31.4	1	50.0	40	37.4
Some previous job most satisfactory	4	9.3	2	7.4	7	20.0	—	—	13	12.1
Total	43	100.0	27	100.0	35	100.0	2	100.0	107	100.0

[1] Replies tabulated only for those who have held some previous job.

TABLE 23

OPINION OF MANAGEMENT BY EMPLOYEES IN THE SAMPLE WORK FORCE, BY PLANTS IN THE SAMPLE

Opinion	Plant A		Plant B		Plant C		Plant D		Total	
	Number	Percent	Number	Percent	Number	Percent	Number	Percent	Number	Percent
Good	32	38.1	20	57.1	22	44.9	12	20.3	86	37.9
Fair	24	28.6	9	25.8	11	22.4	11	18.6	55	24.2
Indifferent	20	23.8	4	11.4	16	32.7	28	47.5	68	29.9
No opinion	8	9.5	2	5.7	—	—	1	1.7	11	4.8
Antagonistic	—	—	—	—	—	—	7	11.9	7	3.2
Total	84	100.0	35	100.0	49	100.0	59	100.0	227	100.0

TABLE 24

OPINION OF MANAGEMENT BY EMPLOYEES IN THE SAMPLE WORK FORCE, BY JOB SKILL

Opinion	Skilled		Semi-skilled		Unskilled		Clerical		Total	
	Number	Percent	Number	Percent	Number	Percent	Number	Percent	Number	Percent
Good	34	53.1	10	23.8	38	33.1	4	66.7	86	37.9
Fair	11	17.2	7	16.7	35	30.4	2	33.3	55	24.2
Indifferent	15	23.4	22	52.4	31	26.9	—	—	68	29.9
No opinion	3	4.7	1	2.4	7	6.1	—	—	11	4.8
Antagonistic	1	1.6	2	4.7	4	3.5	—	—	7	3.2
Total	64	100.0	42	100.0	115	100.0	6	100.0	227	100.0

TABLE 25
OPINION OF MANAGEMENT BY EMPLOYEES IN THE SAMPLE WORK FORCE, BY UNION MEMBERSHIP

Opinion	Member		Non-member		Total	
	Number	Percent	Number	Percent	Number	Percent
Good	29	29.6	37	44.2	86	37.9
Fair	20	20.4	35	27.2	55	24.2
Indifferent	41	41.8	27	20.9	68	29.9
No opinion	2	2.0	9	6.9	11	4.8
Antagonistic	6	6.2	1	0.8	7	3.2
Total	98	100.0	129	100.0	227	100.0

Appendix II: The Survey of the Characteristics of the Work Force in Saigon

by James B. Hendry

THE SURVEY on which Chapter 11 is based was affected by two main types of limitations:

(1) The first of these might be termed general limitations in the sense that the very situation the survey sought to investigate was not conducive to detailed probing. Managements, unions and workers, as a result of Vietnam's recent history, the strains, tensions, and uncertainties of transition from colonial status to independence, and the constant threat posed by subversive elements at all levels of society, are all apt to be suspicious and resentful of outside interviewers whose motives they can not easily understand or believe. The decision was therefore made to use a judgment sample of representative firms whose managements, through personal acquaintance and first-hand knowledge, promised genuine cooperation. This was decided in preference to a random sample where cooperation was less assured. Interviewing is virtually unknown in Vietnam, and most people have neither seen the results of interviews in the form of reported findings nor served as interviewees. The type of questioning they are most likely to be familiar with are all associated with police or security matters, and the climate for interviewing seemed uncertain at best. Questions selected for the questionnaire were kept very general, and avoided matters which might seem threatening or overly personal. Detail was sacrificed in the interest of minimizing suspicion of the purpose of the interview, thereby, it was hoped, increasing the reliability of the answers given to the questions asked. The result of these different compromises was a survey that cannot be used as a random sample of the population it seeks .to measure, and which ignores a number of obvious and interesting questions. At the same time, since the sample was chosen with some care, the findings cannot be discounted completely, for the replies are internally consistent and check well in all cases where benchmark data are available.

(2) The second group of limitations involved resource limitations

essentially. The survey was conducted by staff of the Michigan State University Advisory Group in Vietnam, an organization with contractual responsibility through the United States Operations Mission in Vietnam to assist the National Institute of Administration in expanding and improving its academic and in-service training programs. Research carried out by staff members, with the cooperation of faculty at the National Institute, could draw only upon resources available within the Michigan State University unit. The role of that unit, as well as the financial means available for research purposes, precluded any large-scale surveys, which in any event tend to be regarded as reserved for agencies of the national government. There was the further problem that few Vietnamese have received any training in interview techniques, although some progress is being made in this area by government agencies such as the Institute of Statistics. The Michigan State University unit, however, was able to use the services of two Vietnamese who have earned Master's degrees in sociology from American universities; they prepared the original questionnaire and conducted all the pre-test and final interviews in Vietnamese.

The four firms chosen for the sample were all medium-scale, light industrial plants producing items typical of this kind of industrial production in Vietnam at the present time—plastics, pottery, pharmaceuticals, and printing. After obtaining permission from the management to interview employees at the plant, and on company time, the purpose of the interview was carefully explained to union representatives and plant foremen who, in turn, assisted in explaining the interviews to the employees. Even so, employees at first asked the interviewers questions such as, "Who are you? What organization do you represent? What is the purpose of the interview? Why have you chosen me? What use are these answers to you? Are you connected with the government? What help will you give us with our problems?" The interviewers patiently explained they were making a study for a university, were interested in learning more about the lives and problems of workers in industry, and that they were not seeking to solve specific problems. These questions subsided as the interviews progressed, and the interviewers reported that cooperation from the workers was, on the whole, excellent.

Within each plant interviewers drew a random selection of employees to be interviewed from a roster of each section of the plant. With the exception of Plant A, the largest of the four, this amounted to one-half the total number employed. Prior to this, the original questionnaire was pre-tested in three plants, none of which were included in the final sample. As a result of the pre-test, questions were simplified, made more direct, and greatly reduced in number. In its final form the questionaire took 30 minutes to complete, with variations depending on the individual interviewee and the difficulty in communicating with him. Interviews were conducted in private, away from other workers or supervisory personnel, and employees were assured that replies would be kept confidential and that the questionnaire forms would not be identified with them in any way.

Appendix III: Health Progress in Vietnam

*by Craig S. Lichtenwalner, M.D.**

SIGNIFICANT ADVANCES have been made in the field of public health in the Republic of Vietnam during the past five years. This assessment is based on my personal knowledge of the problem as a result of two and-one-half years of work in that country. In discussing Vietnam's public health problems, accomplishments, and goals, it is appropriate to bear in mind the remarkable achievements that have already been recorded.

With a total population of 13 million, the Republic of Vietnam lies wholly below the 17th parallel in a tropical monsoon area. Besides determining the daily and seasonal activities of the people and the pattern of agriculture, the monsoons also influence both the distribution and prevalence of insect vectors of disease as well as the seasonal variation of certain diseases. Significantly, the major causes of death and disability in Vietnam are the preventable diseases: malaria, trachoma, dysentery, tuberculosis, and a few others. Therefore, with good methods for control of most of these diseases already within our knowledge, it only remains for Vietnam to harness this knowledge within an administrative and organizational framework which can effectively treat and prevent such diseases.

A great measure of the responsibility for those functions is vested within the Department of Health of the Vietnamese Government. In Vietnam the Health Department, with substantially broader functions than those of the United States, is responsible for administering a national health service rendering direct medical care and treatment, including the operation of a network of hospitals. The Department also

---

*Craig S. Lichtenwalner, M.D., is Assistant Dean of the Medical School, American University of Beirut, Beirut, Lebanon. He was formerly with the U. S. Public Health Service on loan to the U. S. Operations Mission to Vietnam.

carries out the more traditional assignments in preventive medicine and public health associated with the activities of governmental agencies in the United States.

Health achievements can be accurately determined by statistics which measure population, births, deaths, and the number of cases of specific illnesses. For a variety of historical and cultural reasons, such statistics on a nation-wide basis are generally unrecorded or of indeterminable reliability in Vietnam. Statistics utilized in this paper are the most recently available, and were provided by the Secretary of State for Health of the Republic of Vietnam in 1959 unless otherwise noted.

ACHIEVEMENTS. One method of demonstrating Vietnam's health achievements over the past five years is through the statistical comparison of budget appropriations, health facilities, health personnel, and services, all of which reveal a dramatic increase.

BUDGET. Because the Department of Health carries such a heavy responsibility for services in Vietnam, the amount of money budgeted for health purpose is important. In 1959, 3.1 per cent of the national budget was allocated to the Department of Health. Proportionately, this is ten times greater than the 1954 figure (0.3 per cent). The increase is even more striking when one considers that the 1954 allocation included sums for North Vietnam, whereas the 1959 figure is solely for the Republic of Vietnam. The national budget, in addition, has increased in size more than forty times over that of 1954, so that the absolute increases in sums allocated for health over the five year period has actually increased almost four hundred fold:

	1954	1959
National Budget	VN$ 3,574,927,000[1]	VN$ 15,276,000,000
Department of Health Budget	12,023,300[1]	472,852,000

[1] Includes North Vietnam
Source: Department of Health

HEALTH FACILITIES. Budgetary increases are reflected in the dramatic increase in the number of hospitals, dispensaries, maternities, and other health facilities over the five year period, as well as in the number of beds available for patient care. The table below illustrates this rise:

	1953[1]		1959[2]		Rate of Increase	
	No.	No. of Beds	No.	No. of Beds	Facilities	Beds
General Hospitals	46	8392	50	10210	9%	22%
Infirmaries and Dispensaries	128	1065	207	1530	62%	43%
Maternities	60	716	480	2055	700%	327%

[1] Includes North Vietnam
[2] For Vietnam south of the 17th parallel; figures as of May 31, 1959

Reflecting the Vietnamese Government's determined policy to extend social services into the villages and provinces, the greatest increase in individual health facilities has taken place in the establishment of maternities, infirmaries, and dispensaries, for the most part small units at the district and village levels. The greatest increase in the number of beds, on the other hand, is in the category of general hospitals which are located in larger population centers. The government has recognized the need to improve existing facilities by initiating a program for the renovation and modernization of buildings and for the provison of new, modern equipment. The establishment of blood banks in Saigon and Hue should also be noted.

HEALTH PERSONNEL. The number of health personnel employed by the Department of Health has also increased substantially over the same period:

	1953[1]	1958[2]
Physicians	130	192
Dentists	10	21
Pharmacists	8	14
Midwives	285	342
Nurses	1174	1659
Assistant Nurses	154	499
Rural Midwives	124	553

[1] Includes North Vietnam
[2] For Vietnam south of the 17th parallel

CARE AND TREATMENT. The increases in budget, facilities, and personnel are reflected in the rise of the activities of the health service:

	1953[1]	1958[2]
Outpatients	2,980,413	4,506,065
Consultations	7,199,620	12,111,536
Inpatients	255,162	269,011
Hospital days	3,123,869	3,953,617

[1] Includes North Vietnam
[2] For Vietnam south of the 17th parallel

ORIENTAL MEDICINE. No account of medical services would be complete without some mention of the practitioners of traditional or oriental medicine, who are everywhere throughout the country. The practitioners are supported by a network of pharmacies carrying oriental medicines. The Statistical Yearbook of Vietnam for 1956 lists the number of practitioners at 1217, and the number of pharmacies at 1679.

PUBLIC HEALTH SERVICES

MALARIA ERADICATION PROGRAM. Malaria is a major health threat in Vietnam, particularly in the uplands regions which heretofore were generally unpopulated by the Vietnamese. The traditional habitat of the primitive *montagnard* tribes, the uplands, in recent years as a result of President Ngo's determined new settlements program has become the new residence for more than 100,000 Vietnamese.

Vietnam has joined many other nations in embarking on a campaign to eradicate malaria on a global basis. Begun in 1957, the total four-phase program planned for Vietnam will require approximately eight years for completion and will involve the expenditure of about nine million dollars.

The initial phase, covering somewhat more than one year, was devoted to surveys, preparation of detailed plans, and personnel training. The second phase, begun in 1959 and expected to require four years, involves the intensive spraying of dwellings with insecticides. By November, 1959, the present campaign had completed the spraying of the millionth dwelling in Vietnam—a remarkable achievement and a demonstration of the intensity with which the government is pursuing its goals.

Upon completion of the spraying, the third phase—surveillance or consolidation—will be undertaken. Its goal is to eliminate all remaining reservoirs of infection through case finding and the utilization of anti-malarial drugs. Malaria eradication is considered to have been achieved when three years of surveillance indicates no locally contracted new cases. At this point the final phase of maintenance will begin. Such maintenance of a malaria-free condition is a normal and relatively inexpensive function of the regular health service.

CONTROL OF EPIDEMICS. The region in which Vietnam is located is historically associated with the great epidemic diseases of cholera, plague, and smallpox. Surprising progress has been made by Vietnam in the control of these diseases, although one should recall that history teaches us not to become overconfident when dealing with

these scourges. Vietnam has, nevertheless, witnessed a sharp reduction
in the incidence of these diseases:

	1953[1]		1959[2]	
	Cases	Deaths	Cases	Deaths
Smallpox	1582	704	12	3
Plague	22	2	0	0
Cholera	3	3	0	0

[1] Includes North Vietnam
[2] For Vietnam south of the 17th parallel; to July 1, 1959

It only remains to be noted that these accomplishments were brought
about chiefly by government-supported programs of immunization and
an active quarantine service.

NUTRITION. Rice, of course, is the mainstay of the Vietnamese
diet. It accounts for at least three-fourths of the total calories consumed
and is the chief source of dietary protein.

The principal source of animal protein is fish, both marine and fresh
water varieties. And, of course, fish is the base from which *nuoc mam*,
the universal and characteristic fish sauce, is made. The chief meats
consumed are pork and poultry. A wide variety of vegetables and fruits
are eaten in season.

It is difficult to arrive at a definite conclusion with respect to the
nutritional status of the Vietnamese at this time because of the absence
of authoritative data. During the war and immediate post-war period,
when rice fields were untilled and there were interruptions in the distribution of foodstuffs, many people lived at a subsistence level and
cases of beri-beri and severe malnutrition were common. At the present
time the situation is much different; one seldom sees in Vietnam cases
of frank malnutrition caused by lack of food.

There are still, however, cases of beri-beri, a disease caused by lack
of vitamin B. The custom of consuming highly polished rice is a major
factor that contributes to the low intake of vitamin B. Another defici-
ency disease, goiter, caused by lack of iodine in the diet, is found in
the highlands regions.

At present a nutritional survey is being carried out in Vietnam by
the Department of Health in cooperation with the United States Interdepartmental Committee on Nutrition, the results of which will enable
the Vietnamese government to undertake a rational campaign to solve
the problem.

Substantial progress has also been made by the government in tuberculosis control, maternal and child health activities and the new Chil-

dren's Hospital, measures for the control of opium addiction, the development of rural health units, drilling of wells for pure water, and improvements in environmental sanitation. Unfortunately, space does not permit their elucidation.

TRAINING OF PERSONNEL. Vietnam's needs for health personnel are great, and one of the major functions of the Department of Health is its training program for many categories of personnel. The shortage of doctors is a major health problem, but this is dealt with in Chapter 5 in connection with medical education.

The Midwife School, the Health Technicians School, and the Nursing School, each with branches in both Hue and Saigon, are major sources for sorely needed trained personnel. Less well-known, but also significant, are the schools for pharmacist assistants and for laboratory technicians. In addition, the Department has conducted a number of courses for other types of personnel: district health workers, assistant nurses, rural midwives, malaria workers, sanitation agents, and others.

The Department has also sent personnel abroad for advanced training in their specialties. About forty members of the Department have been sent to foreign countries for long-term training (a year or more) and many more have gone for shorter terms.

INTERNATIONAL ACTIVITIES. In the realm of international activities, Vietnam has been an active participant in international health affairs. Each year official delegations are sent to important international meetings and congresses. In the past five years, Vietnam has been represented at 47 international conferences in the field of health.

In 1958, at the Eleventh World Health Assembly which was held in Minneapolis, Vietnam was elected to the Executive Board of the World Health Organization for a three-year term, and the Secretary of State for Health, Dr. Tran Vy, was elected a vice president of the Assembly.

FUTURE GOALS

Having completed this brief survey of the Republic of Vietnam's achievements during its first five years, it is appropriate now to list some of the goals that the Department of Health has established for itself, as recorded in the Department's Health Yearbook published in 1958.

An overall goal set by the Department is to reach a ratio of two hospital beds per 1000 population, as compared with the United States ratio of more than 8 beds per thousand.

Other plans call for enlargement of the National Cancer Institute; renovation of the Central Pharmacy; completion of a drug control laboratory; increasing the number of trained personnel—physicians, dentists, pharmacists, nurses, midwives, and so on; and modernizing and replacing the medical and scientific equipment in hospitals. Of course, achieving these goals will depend on the budgetary support granted to the Department.

PROBLEMS

Finally, consideration should be given to some of the major problems which the Department of Health will face in the future:

HEALTH STATISTICS. Achievements in the health field can be approximated in many ways but they can be measured only by accurate statistics. The Department of Health already possesses a statistical office, but it is handicapped by the lack of a well-developed reporting system. A central office can process only the data that are sent to it. It is necessary to further develop the reporting system for births, deaths, illnesses, and other health data so that it will reach into every village and hamlet.

PLAN FOR EXPANSION. A second major requirement is the development by the Department of Health of a systematic plan for the expansion of health services, with special emphasis given to the problems of providing administrative and technical support to the health units at the district and village levels. Such a plan might also envisage the task of better coordinating and using to better advantage the technical and material aid offered by international agencies and friendly nations.

Parenthetically, I might add that these organizations and agencies, public and private, might stop to consider the administrative problems that the Department of Health must face in dealing with them. There are a least five major, and three times as many minor, organizations, agencies, and countries that have contacts with the Department. Each has its own bureaucratic peculiarities—its own forms, its own fiscal year, its own policies, and its own representatives. To deal with them all effectively is a formidable administrative task.

UPGRADING OF FACILITIES AND PERSONNEL. Third, I would like to reemphasize the necessity for upgrading existing health facilities and personnel. There is a qualitative factor as well as a quantitative one that must be considered when we analyze numbers of health facilities, beds or health personnel.

In regard to patient beds in health facilities, for example, many of these beds could not be considered adequate by the system of hospital standards of more developed countries. From the standpoint of personnel, nurses are of necessity sometimes serving where there should be doctors, assistant nurses where there should be nurses, and so on.

In listing the above problems, there is no implication that these are necessarily the only nor the most important problems facing the Department of Health. Likewise, there is no implication that these problems are not known to the Department. On the contrary, the problems are fully appreciated and are receiving attention.

SUMMARY

This brief presentation has dealt with the highlights of health achievements in Vietnam during the past five years. Examples have been given of some of the accomplishments and some of the problems that remain.

There is no question that significant progress has been made, and one may be confident that real progress will continue to be made in the future.

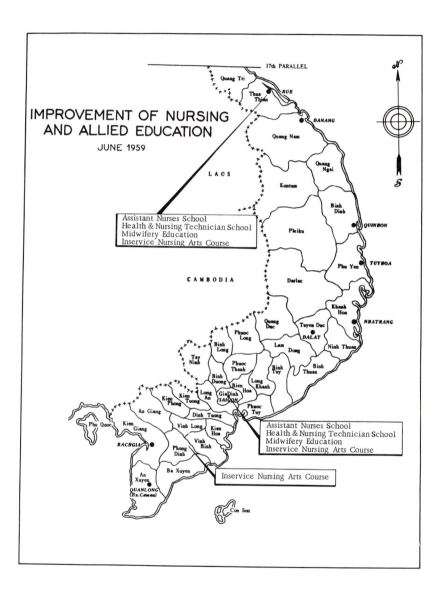

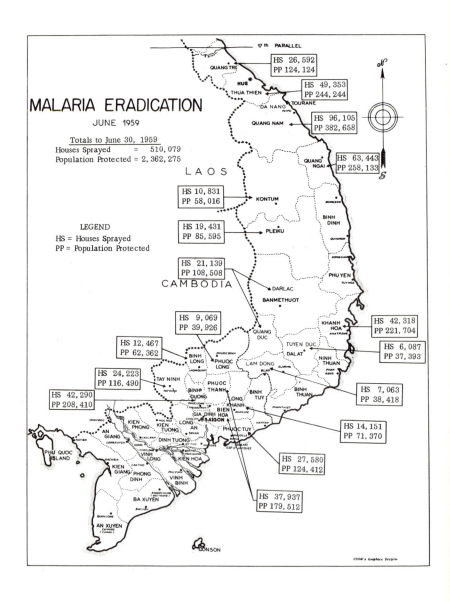

MALARIA ERADICATION

JUNE 1959

Totals to June 30, 1959
Houses Sprayed = 510,079
Population Protected = 2,362,275

LEGEND
HS = Houses Sprayed
PP = Population Protected

Index

A

Administrative system, 139-152; basic changes in, 139-142
Administrators, lack of trained, 12
Agrarian reform, 71, 153-176, 181; Cai San Resettlement Project, 126, 163, 184; Council on, 168; land transfer, 170; National Committee for, 158; Ordinances 2 and 7, 159, 160, 162; Ordinance 57, 167-168; Tenants' Union, 161
Agricultural credit and cooperatives, 47, 177-189; Agricultural Cooperative of Bac Giang, 178; General Commissariats for, 146; Native Societies for Mutual Agricultural Credit, 178, 180; Workshop, 186
Agricultural development, 126; in favor of industrialization, 70
American Aid Funds, 180
Annam, 3, 5, 9, 148
Anti-Four Vices Campaign, 29, 33
d'Argenlieu, Admiral, 9
Army, National, 13

B

Baclieu, 155
Bao, Nguyen Huy, 41, 53, 55
Bell, Daniel, 63
Berdyaev, 35
Binh Xuyen, 12, 13, 30, 160
Bon, Ly, 113
Books and libraries, 93
Buber, 35
Buddhism, 41, 57
Budget and Foreign Aid, General Directorate of, 145
Buttinger, Joseph, 99

C

Cai San Resettlement Project; see Agrarian reform

Cambodians, 99
Can-Lao Party, 48, 60, 150
Can, Huy Cu, 59
Can, Ngo Dinh, 25
Cantho, 155
Cao Dai, 12, 13, 30, 58, 160
Chams, 99
Changes and stress in administration, 139-152
Chiang Kai-Shek, 113
Chieu, Ngo Van, 58
Chinese: assimilation of, 109-119; Bangs, 116; Congregations, 116-117; Decree No. 53, 110; education of, 95; Minh Huong, 114, 116; Nanking Convention, 117; Ordinance 48, 110; Tayson revolution, 114; Treaty of Chunking, 118
Chungking, Treaty of, see Chinese
Civic Action, General Commissariats for, 146; teams, 49
Civil Service, 76
Cochinchina, 2, 9, 148, 154
Collectivization, 36
Community development, 47
Communist influence on land distribution, 153, 157
Confucianism, 33, 43, 55; revival of, 31-34
Cong Hoa Youth Movement, 48
Congress of Women Civil Servants, 51
Constitution of Republic, description of, 22; preamble to, 34
Cooperative Research and Training Center, 187
Cooperatives, see Agricultural credit and cooperatives
Cooperatives, Union of, 178
Council on Agrarian Reform, see Agrarian reform
Cras, M., 53
Cu Huy Can, 59

D

Dai, Bao, 12, 14, 16, 157, 158, 163
Dai Viet party, 15
Dan, Phan Quang, 15
De, Prince Cuong, 14
Decoux, Admiral, 9
Democratic growth, 9-29
Development, Vietnam's concept of, 69-75
Dich, Tran Muc, 49
Dieu, Xuan, 59
Domaine Agricole de l'Ouest, 155
Dong Minh Hoi, 15
Donnell, John C., 29
Dorsey, John T., Jr., 139
Dru, Gilbert, 36
Duc, Tu, 103-104
Duong, Buu, 53

E

Economie et Humanisme, 37
Economic development: balanced growth principle, 72; changes in, 6; foreign-domestic market, 71; French firms and businessmen, 3; Geneva result on, 3; internal trade, 3; military effect on, 6; refugees, their effect on, 5; regions of, 2; restructuring, difficulties of, 4; war, effect of years of, 4
Education, 75-97; administrative problems, state universities, 90; books and libraries, difficulties with, 93; changes and expansion, 77-78; character of students, 78; of Chinese residents, 95; Confucian system, 75; diploma as status symbol, 78-80; elementary and secondary, 84; enrollment, 85; evolution of system, 91; foreign aid to, 96; French system, 76; higher education, 87-90 (*see also* Universities); illiteracy, 90; language problem, 82; Mandarin system, 76; methods of teaching, 90; origins, 75; personnel, lack of, 81, 96; policies and aims, 80; Quoc Tu Giam, 76; reforms, 81; specialization, 89; train-

ing abroad, 94; teachers, 92; technical, 85; Tran Hu The, 77; University of Dalat, 88-89; University of Hue, 87-88; University of Saigon, *see* Saigon, University of; USOM, 83-96
Emerson, Rupert, 141
Epidemics, control of, 222
Esprit, 34, 57
Ethnic minorities, 99-121; Cambodians, 99; Chams, 99; Chinese, assimilation of, 109-119; *Montagnards,* 101-109
Existentialists, 35

F

Family Bill, 50-51
Family formation, 192
Farmers' Association, 187
Farmers' Union, 47
Foreign Aid to education, 96
Finance and Justice, Department of, 146
French Christian Democratic movement, 36, 37, 58
French colony, Cochinchina as, 9
Fishel, Wesley R., 9

G

Geneva Conference, 3, 10-11
Greene, Graham, 43
Growth, Vietnam's developmental view of, 69

H

Health: diseases major cause of death, 219; Oriental medicine, 220
Health, Department of: budget, 220; goals, 224; expansion plans of, 225; facilities, 220; personnel, 221, and training program for, 224; progress and achievements, 219-226; services: care and treatment, 221; epidemic control, 222; international activities, 224; malaria eradication, 222; health statistics, 225; nutrition, 223
Henderson, William, 123
Hendry, James B., 191, 216

Hinh, Nguyen Van, 13, 19
Hoa-Hao, 12, 13, 30, 160
Hoa, Nguyen Dinh, 89
Hue, University of, 87-88
Huu, Tran Van

I

Illiteracy, 90
Indian Rig Veda, 41
Indochinese Office for Mutual Agricultural Credit, 178
Industrial employment, workers' attitude toward, 200-203
Industrialization, national policy in relation to agriculture, 70
Information Department, 42
Institut Taberd, 84
Intelligentsia, 26

J

Japanese occupation, 1
Jaspers, 35

K

Kherian, Professor, 178
Kuhn, Ferdinand, 119

L

Labor associations, 197-199
Ladejinský, Wolf, 153
Land development program, 123-137; accomplishments, 136; aid and assistance for, 128; areas, 127; Commissariat General for Agricultural Development, 123, 126, 133, 146; facilities, 132; Highlands project, 72; resettlement program, 130-132
Land redistribution program, 155
Land tenure system, 154
Language problem, 82
League of Revolutionary Civil Servants, 42, 149-150
Lebret, Father Louis, 37
Libraries, 93
Lichtenwalner, Craig S., M.D., 219
Lien, Tran Ngoc, 177

Loi, Emperor Le, 54
London Personalist Group, 38
Long, Gia, 115, 116
Luan, Father Cao Van, 89
Luong, Bui Van, 126
Luzzatti, Luigi, 186

M

Malaria Eradication Program, 222
Mang, Minh, 115, 116, 117
Marcel, Gabriel, 35
Maritain, Jacques, 29, 34, 36
Marxist materialism, 35
Michigan State University Advisory Group, 217
Minh, Ho Chi, 30
Ministry of National Economy, 33
Montagnards, 101-109, 125, 130, 131, 134; Champa kingdom of, 102; present activity concerning, 107; present condition of, 105
Morality campaigns, 31-34
Mo-ti, 41
Mounier, Emmanuel, 29, 34-36, 38, 41
Movement républican populaire (MRP), 36

N

National Service of Agriculture, 178, 180
Native Societies for Mutual Agricultural Credit, 178, 180
Nicolson, Harold, 19-20
Ngo Dinh Diem, 11, 13, 15, 16, 18, 19, 21, 23-24, 27, 29, 32, 34, 37-39, 41, 46-47, 56, 57, 63, 112, 118, 126, 159, 161, 165, 172-174, 184, 188, 222
Nhu, Ngo Dinh, 25, 30, 34, 37, 40, 43, 46, 48, 54, 56
Nhu, Mme Ngo Dinh, 50, 51
Nguyen Van Tam, 13, 158, 165
Nutrition, United States Interdepartmental Committee of, 223

P

Paliard, Jacques, 49

Partition, consequences of, 1-8
Pasquier, Governor General, 180
Personalism in Vietnam, 29-65; doctrine, official statements of, 38-42; in education, 52; European influence on, 34-38; formulations of, 42; "Historical Mission," 54; morality campaigns and Confucianism, 31-34; Personalism Training Center, 31, 42, 49; Personalist Revolutionary Labor Party, *see Can-Lao* Party; political action, 49
Pike, Edgar N., 75
Political development, background of, 14
Popular Credit Office, 178
Population, occupational characteristics of, 5
Provincial Banks for Mutual Agricultural Credit, 178
Public health; *see* Department of Health

Q

Quat, Phan Huy, 15
Quoc Dan Dang [Vietnam Nationalist Party], 15
Quoc Tu Giam, 76
Quynh, Pham, 31, 32

R

Radio Hanoi, 109, 172
Republican Party, 15
Revolutionary Personalist Labor Party; *see Can-Lao* Party
Revolutionary Workers' Party for Human Dignity; *see Can-Lao* Party
Riggs, Fred W., 141
Roy, Rammohun, 58

S

Saigon, University of: administrative problems in, 89-90; composition of, 88; contributions of French cultural mission to, 97; Law Faculty of, 145; as National University of Vietnam, 87; as Université Mixte Franco-Vietnamienne, 87

Social Solidarity Movement, 51
Social structure, creation of new, 72-73

T

Taberd, Institut, 84
Tax Directorate, 148
Tayson Revolution, 114
Technical Center, at Phu Tho, 85
Tenancy, 156-157
Tenants' Union, 161
Thai, Vu Van, 69
Thanh, Tran Huu, 45
The, Tran Huu, 52, 77, 81
Thich, Nguyen Van, 53
Thomism, 35, 42
Thuc, Ngo Dinh, 30, 49, 165
Times of Vietnam, 32, 33, 51, 53
Tinh-Than [Spirit] Group, 48
Tinh Viet literary group, 43
Tonkin, 3, 5, 9, 148
Tran Muc Dich, 49
Tran Ngoc Lien, 177
Trinh, Lam Le, 42
Trinh, Nguyen Quang, 87
Tu, Nguyen Van, 58
Tuan, Bui, 43
Tru, Father Phero Nguyen, 49

U

Union membership of labor force in Saigon, 196-200, 213, 214
Union of Cooperatives, 178
United States: Interdepartmental Committee on Nutrition, 223; Operations Mission, 127, 128, 132-134, 187, 191, 217

V

Vietnam Confucian Association, 33
Viet Cong, 17, 21
Viet Minh, 29, 53, 54, 109, 124, 149, 161, 175, 178
Viet Nam Duy Tan Hoi [Association for the Modernization of Vietnam], 14

Viet Nam Phuc Quoc Hoi [Vietnam Restoration Party], 14

Vietnam Nationalist Party; *see Quoc Dan Dang*

Vietnam Press, 32, 42

Vietnam Revolutionary League; *see Dong Minh Hoi*

Vietnamese Veterans' Association, 24

Vy, Dr. Tran, 224

W

Work force in Saigon, 191-205; adult population, 208-209; attitudes of, 200-203; domicile of family unit, 209; education, 212; employment, previous, 211; geographical origins of, 193-196; incomes of, 193, 209; job skills of, 208, 212; job satisfaction of, 214; job tenure of, 210; opinion of management, 202, 215; reasons for staying, 213; Saigon-born, 211; sex distribution of, 207, 208; impact of unions on, 196-200; union membership of, 213, 214

World Health Organization, 224

X

Xuan Dieu, 59